CIM REVISION CARDS

Managing Marketing Performance

Mike Willoughby of Marketing Knowledge

ELSEVIER

AMSTERDAM • BOSTON • HEIDELBERG • LONDON • NEW YORK • OXFORD
PARIS • SAN DIEGO • SAN FRANCISCO • SINGAPORE • SYDNEY • TOKYO

Butterworth-Heinemann is an imprint of Elsevier

Butterworth-Heinemann is an imprint of Elsevier
Linacre House, Jordan Hill, Oxford OX2 8DP
30 Corporate Drive, Suite 400, Burlington, MA 01803

First published 2008

Permissions may be sought directly from Elsevier's Science & Technology Rights Department in Oxford, UK: phone: (+44) (0) 1865 843830; fax: (+44) (0) 1865 853333, e-mail: permissions @ elsevier.co.uk. You may also complete your request on-line via the Elsevier homepage (http://www.elsevier.com), by selecting 'Customer Support' and then 'Obtaining Permissions'.

British Library Cataloguing in Publication Data
A catalogue record for this book is available from the British Library

ISBN-13: 978-0-7506-8643-3

For information on all Butterworth-Heinemann publications visit our web site at http://books.elsevier.com

Printed and bound in Spain

08 09 10 10 9 8 7 6 5 4 3 2 1

TABLE OF CONTENTS

PREFACE

Welcome to the CIM Revision Cards from Elsevier/Butterworth–Heinemann. We hope you will find these useful to revise for your CIM exam. The cards are designed to be used in conjunction with the CIM Coursebooks from Elsevier/Butterworth–Heinemann, and have been written specifically with revision in mind. They also serve as invaluable reviews of the complete modules, perfect for those studying via the assignment route.

■ Learning outcomes at the start of each chapter identify the main points

■ Key topics are summarised, helping you commit the information to memory quickly and easily

■ Examination and revision tips are provided to give extra guidance when preparing for the exam

■ Key diagrams are featured to aid the learning process

■ The compact size ensures the cards are easily transportable, so you can revise any time, anywhere.

To get the most of your revision cards, try to look over them as frequently as you can when taking your CIM course. When read alongside the Coursebook they serve as the ideal companion to the main text. Good luck – we wish you every success with your CIM qualification!

MANAGING MARKETING PERFORMANCE

Introduction

SUMMARY

➡ When studying and revising for this module, it is helpful to be aware of the context of the module within the Professional Post-graduate Diploma Syllabus

➡ Whilst the Strategic Marketing Decisions Module is, as its name implies, intended to deal with the formulation of strategy, the topics surrounding the creation of an environment in which that strategy can be effectively developed and implemented are covered in this module

➡ It is worthwhile, therefore, to take a few minutes to study the overview of the units on the following page to see how they relate to each other and how they are relevant to the marketing function of an organization

➡ The module covers topics such as team building to ensure that organizations have the people capabilities to develop and implement strategies. It covers the management of change because the implementation of strategy implies change. It also covers a range of broader management techniques that are required by marketers either directly or in the course of their interactions with other functions within the organization.

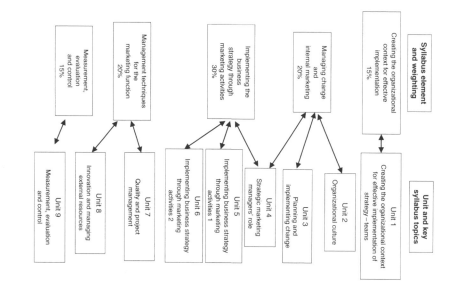

Syllabus element and weighting	Unit and key syllabus topics
Creating the organizational context for effective implementation 15%	Unit 1 Creating the organizational context for effective implementation of strategy – teams
Managing change and internal marketing 20%	Unit 2 Organizational culture
	Unit 3 Planning and implementing change
	Unit 4 Strategic marketing managers' role
Implementing the business strategy through marketing activities 30%	Unit 5 Implementing business strategy through marketing activities 1
	Unit 6 Implementing business strategy through marketing activities 2
Management techniques for the marketing function 20%	Unit 7 Quality and project management
	Unit 8 Innovation and managing external resources
Measurement, evaluation and control 15%	Unit 9 Measurement, evaluation and control

CREATING THE ORGANIZATIONAL CONTEXT

LEARNING OUTCOMES

9.63.1 Critically evaluate the techniques available for integrating teams and activities across the organization, specifically relating to brands and customer-facing processes, and instilling learning within the organization.

1.1 Appraise the requirements of a given set of tasks and their context, and assess the impact of relevant factors on the creation or development of a team to perform those tasks.

1.2 Determine the skills, characteristics and roles required within a team to carry out specific tasks effectively.

1.3 Prepare a plan showing how the team should be structured, selected, formed and developed to ensure effective performance.

LEARNING OUTCOMES – CONTINUED

1.4 Lead the work of individuals and teams to achieve their objectives and create effective working relationships both within their team and with other teams.

1.5 Critically evaluate the productivity, satisfaction and effectiveness of teams against their objectives using appropriate techniques.

1.6 Analyse the causes of any sub-optimal performance and recommend how to improve the team's performance, including plans to improve motivation, commitment and loyalty.

Syllabus References: 9.63, 1.1–1.6

Teams

This unit relates to the role that marketing can play in creating an organizational environment that supports an effective implementation of the strategy developed in the Strategic Marketing Decisions Course Module.

■ The unit calls on the concept of the Learning Organization, which is also relevant to Unit 8. Whilst individuals acquire knowledge, it is important to make this knowledge available where it is needed within the organization. At a more sophisticated level, individuals develop mental models; by sharing these across the organization, processes, particularly those involving, for example, innovation can become more efficient and effective.

■ Logically, the starting point for organizational team building is a definition of the task or tasks to be performed.

■ It is then important to consider the current position in terms of skills and resources, as these will impact on the options that the organization has. Gaps may be identified at this stage.

■ The unit then considers how teams may be created, developed and managed effectively, often using groups of individuals as a starting point. In doing this, the importance of Leadership is also considered.

KEY DEFINITIONS

A team – is a small number of people with complementary skills who are committed to a common purpose, performance goals and approach for which they hold themselves mutually accountable (Katzenbach and Smith, 1994).

Work roles – may be defined as, 'The mix of tasks and responsibilities undertaken by individuals or executed within teams' (Belbin, 2004).

Virtual teams – may be considered as 'geographically virtual' where team members are not physically located in relatively close proximity, or 'temporally virtual' separated by time either due to two or three shifts occurring in the working day, or due to shifts in time zones in global organizations.

Team roles – characteristic behaviour patterns ascribed to team members. The objective is to ensure a good balance of different team role types depending on the requirements of the project to ensure complementarity and to maximise team performance.

Gantt charts – a graphical technique for displaying work sequences, usually for a project.

Strategic choice theory – makes a distinction between formulation of strategy and its implementation. The formulation of strategy includes preparing a plan, the intended actions required to achieve plan objectives and forecasts the consequences of those actions. Implementation is the procedure of designing systems to ensure that plans are carried out (Stacey, 2003, p. 51).

Theory of the learning organization – is the basis of an outstanding organization when it is able to tap the commitment and capacity of its members to learn. Such learning is particularly effective in teams (Senge (1990) cited in Stacey (2003), p. 51).

Tasks

Projects, large or small, can be broken down into tasks, about each of which certain information is required.

Task characteristics

■ Be measurable in terms of cost, effort, resource and time.

■ Result in a single (verifiable) end product.

■ Have clear start and end dates.

■ Be the responsibility of a single person.

Source: Brown, M., 2002

Task information

■ Description of task

■ Necessary inputs or preconceptions

■ Deliverables

■ Particular resource requirements (with costs)

■ Particular skill requirements

■ Responsibilities

■ Estimated time

Source: Brown, M., 2002

Team roles and contributions

Belbin concluded that there were only certain ways that people could contribute to teamwork and he used these on which to base his team roles.

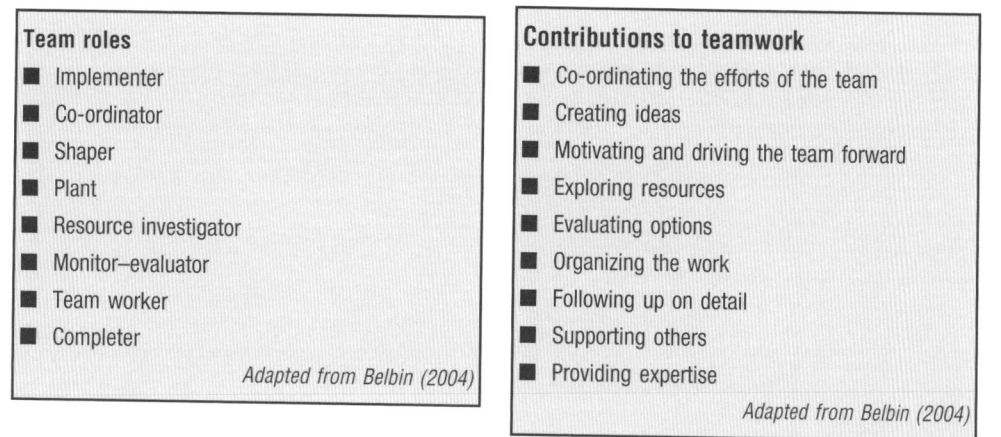

Team roles
- Implementer
- Co-ordinator
- Shaper
- Plant
- Resource investigator
- Monitor–evaluator
- Team worker
- Completer

Adapted from Belbin (2004)

Contributions to teamwork
- Co-ordinating the efforts of the team
- Creating ideas
- Motivating and driving the team forward
- Exploring resources
- Evaluating options
- Organizing the work
- Following up on detail
- Supporting others
- Providing expertise

Adapted from Belbin (2004)

Stages in team development

Adapted from Tuckman (1977)

Forming

Everyone in the embryonic team is yet to feel emotionally attached to it. Members tend to feel a certain degree of anxiety as roles and relationships within the team are established. Group members make an initial assessment of interpersonal relationships and norms within the group and on identification and characteristics of tasks.

Norming

In this stage, group bonding, team spirit and cohesion develop. Level of commitment to each other, and to the team, increases. People feel sure about their team identity and role. Group norms develop. Problems over the demands of particular tasks, and task allocation, have been resolved and conflict diminishes.

Storming

In this phase people understand their function within the team and team relationships settle. Sub-groups may start to form leading to potential for conflict as group members begin to know each other. There may be some conflict not only over leadership but also over how the leader will operate.

Performing

The team has fully committed to achieving its goals. They are flexible and collaborate freely and willingly. Now that people feel comfortable with each other and their work role, they can devote a substantial amount of emotional, as well as physical, energy to the project. Creativity thrives.

Evaluating teams

The characteristics of high-performing teams

Adapted from Wheelan (1999)

- Members are clear about, and agree with, team goals.
- Members are clear about the role they are asked to play; have the ability, and skills necessary, to accept, agree to and accomplish the assigned or chosen task.
- High degree of interdependence exists, as many team tasks require co-operation.
- The leader's style changes as necessary to meet group needs as they arise.
- A very open communications structure (people as well as systems) facilitates the participation and contribution of all members of the team who can provide constructive feedback to each other with the focus on individual performance.
- Time is spent initially on planning and reaching consensus on how decisions are to be made and problems will be solved.
- Team solutions and decisions are implemented and they have in place methods by which implementation of decisions is evaluated. This results in rapid detection of poor decisions or indeed poor implementation.
- Norms of behaviours encourage creative and innovative performance.
- Suitable structure – as small as is possible to achieve objectives. Sub-groups are encouraged and are not seen as threatening.
- Highly cohesive with co-operative members who can accommodate conflict.

Motivation theories

Table 1.1.

Herzberg (1996)	Suggested that people are motivated to work in co-operation with others by both extrinsic motivators, such as money, and intrinsic motivators, such as recognition for achievement, responsibility, advancement and personal growth.
Maslow (1954)	Maslow in his hierarchy of needs (see CIM Stage 2) suggested that when an organization creates conditions in which people can satisfy their 'self-actualisation' needs (the highest level in his hierarchy of needs), then they are powerfully motivated to work for the good of the team and of the organization.
Schein (1988)	One of the several authors to consider three categories of relationships. These are 'coercive', where individuals only do the bare minimum to evade punishment and 'utilitarian' where the individual does enough simply to earn the desired level of reward. The final category is a 'normative' form of relationship where individuals value what they are doing for its own sake, as they believe in it. In this situation the individual's ideology matches that of the organization and this acts as the highest level of individual motivation for the benefit of the organization.

Developing teams

Moxon (1994) suggests that teambuilding involves the following:

- Regular meetings to establish and review processes, procedures and objectives. Effectiveness will decline if this is not undertaken.

- Sessions specifically on addressing issues. Strengths and the causes of successes are examined rather than simply focusing on weaknesses and their causes. The focus is on workable solutions.

- Ongoing emphasis on encouraging open and honest discussion rather than superficial politeness. This requires the creation of a sense of security within the team where team members feel able to take risks and share their deeper and true feelings.

- A commitment to personal change and development and to change to improve team performance. Change will be detailed in action plans and these will also be subject to review.

- Frequent time away from the job, especially in the early stages of team formation, in support of team development.

- Openness of the leader to receive feedback from the team on leadership style and effectiveness.

- Development of interpersonal skills, especially with regard to processes (e.g. meetings) and relationships. This normally should take place as a team.

Revision tips

- Building teams and improving performance is an important element of the syllabus and one that can be examined in a number of contexts.

- The building and effective management of teams should be recognised as a process. Like any other process the way that it is managed makes a contribution to both its effectiveness and its efficiency (see Unit 7).

- It is extremely important to relate theory to practice. Take time to consider how you approach tasks and assemble a group of people to tackle them. How does their performance improve as the individuals in the group grow to understand each other and work together effectively?

- Adopting a slightly different viewpoint, consider the different role of individuals in teams of which you have been a member. How have the ways in which those individuals have fitted those roles affected the performance of the team?

- Motivation is also important in determining individual and organizational performance. Again, test the various theories by using them to attack motivational problems and see how well each one enables the problem to be diagnosed and a solution found.

MANAGING CHANGE AND INTERNAL MARKETING

LEARNING OUTCOMES

9.63.2 Identify the barriers to effective implementation of strategies and plans involving change (including communications) in the organization, and develop measures to prevent or overcome them.

2.1 Recommend how an organization should become more strongly market oriented, taking into account the nature of its environment and culture.

2.2 Assess the main pressures on an organization to change, the sources of any resistance to change and the current change iniatives that organizations are using to respond.

Syllabus References: 9.63.2, 2.1, 2.2

Organizational culture

- This unit and Unit 3 address the effect of organizational culture on performance and how change in that culture can be achieved in order to improve performance.

- This unit deals specifically with the different cultural orientations of organizations and the external pressures that dictate the appropriateness of that culture.

- We need to take account not just of the orientation and culture of the organization, but also that of the individuals, particularly in an international context, and how cross-cultural differences can present barriers to implementation of strategy.

- In doing this, we also consider the ways in which the external environment may be interpreted and the implications for an organization's performance.

Market Orientation – Market Orientation entails: one or more departments engaging in activities geared towards developing an understanding of customers' current and future needs and the factors affecting them; sharing of this understanding across departments and the various departments engaging in activities designed to meet select customer needs (Kohli and Jaworski, 1990).

Culture – Aaker (1998) suggested that organizational culture involves three elements: (1) A set of shared values or dominant beliefs that define an organization's priorities; (2) A set of norms of behaviour and (3) Symbols and symbolic activities used to develop and nurture those shared values and norms.

Strategic fit – This is where the organization's strategy is aligned with the marketing environment in which it operates. Many marketers use the analogy of the organization being like an animal that attempts to be in harmony with its environment. In the case of the organization this is aligned with the customers that it serves.

Environmental scanning – (A) 'The process of monitoring and analysing the marketing environment of a company' (Jobber, 2001, p. 142). (B) 'The process by which environmental stimuli are selected and organized into patterns which are meaningful to the organization in the light of its current and future needs and interests' (Brownlie).

Marketing environment – 'Consists of the actors and forces that affect a company's capability to operate effectively in providing products and services to its customers.'

Market orientation

There are many cultural aspects to an organization. One of the most fundamental is the focus of managerial efforts and resources – its orientation. Whilst a focus on production, sales or benefits to society can be viewed as viable, the pace of change in organizations' markets dictates that at least some, and often a considerable, element of market orientation is necessary for long-term survival.

Piercy (2002) argues for a distinction between market and marketing orientation. A focus on the function of marketing is no longer appropriate – what is required is a focus on the market itself and, in particular, the customer.

Kohli and Jaworski (1990) identified that a market orientation entails

■ One or more departments engaging in activities geared towards developing an understanding of customers' current and future needs and the factors affecting them;

■ Sharing of this understanding across departments; and

■ The various departments engaging in activities designed to meet select customer needs.

However, as will be seen on the following page, an organizations' awareness must encompass a number of aspects to achieve a sustainable long-term profit focus.

A model of market orientation

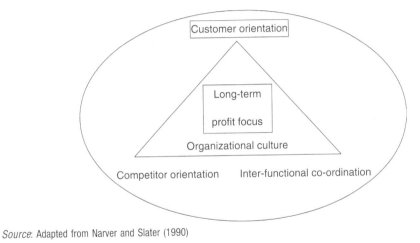

Source: Adapted from Narver and Slater (1990)

Going to market

Nigel Piercy (2002) identifies a number of differences between marketing and 'going to market', suggesting that mangers should focus on the three key issues of Customers, Market strategy and Implementation.

- Strategies are based on customers and markets
- Internal processes of change and external actions are driven by those strategies
- Relationships are fundamental (customers, competitors and intermediaries)
- Information technology underpins new ways of doing business.
- Emphasis is on delivering a customer-focused strategy

Piercy suggests that organizations need to respond to the following new challenges:

New customer demands and expectations – customer expectations are increasing and they are less willing to accept second-class service

New competitors – competition is coming not just from established competitors but also from new entrants, such as the entrance of Virgin into financial services and EasyJet into car rental

New types of organizations being established – many organizations are downsizing and becoming more narrowly focused. Others (such as Time Warner and AOL) are entering strategic alliances and collaborative partnerships

Whole **new ways of doing business** are being developed – for example, e-Marketing.

Organizational culture

The culture of an organization may be classified in a number of ways. Deal & Kennedy (2000) suggest doing so on the basis of attitude to risk

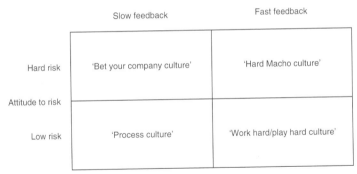

Speed of feedback

	Slow feedback	Fast feedback
Hard risk	'Bet your company culture'	'Hard Macho culture'
Attitude to risk		
Low risk	'Process culture'	'Work hard/play hard culture'

Handy suggests that the culture of an organization depends on what or who is viewed as important within the organization.

Power culture – with the owner manager/ entrepreneur acting with complete authority. Such people are risk takers and tend to see administrative processes and procedures as getting in the way. They, rather than the organizational systems and procedures that legitimise action in larger, long-established organizations, are the source of power.

Role culture – organizations are highly bureaucratic with people specialising on a functional basis. Order, predictability and hierarchy are important. Procedures, rules and regulations for them define the essence of the organization and adherence to these is the essence of 'good' management.

Task culture – as the name suggests, is highly focused on work, whether it is in terms of general work function and/or particular projects with which people are involved.

Person culture – where personal goals, satisfaction and interest drive organizational behaviour. This is most commonly manifested in organizations and divisions where technical specialists predominate – for example accountants, lawyers and so on. They see their work as a vehicle for personal expression rather than simply getting the job done.

The influence of national culture

Hofstede identifies five dimensions which account for cross-cultural differences in belief systems and values:

1. **Individualism v Collectivism** – in the United States and United Kingdom, for example, differences and individualism are admired. In China, for example, conformity is the norm.

2. **Masculinity v Femininity** – in the United States and Japan, for example, masculinity and assertiveness is admired and the less assertive are viewed negatively. The opposite holds in, for example, Denmark and Sweden.

3. **Power v Distance** – in France and India, for example, superiors display and exercise power. In Denmark, for example, members of society feel more equal.

4. **Uncertainty Avoidance** – in Denmark and Sweden, for example, people accept a reasonable level of ambiguity and uncertainty. In Japan and France, these would be viewed as threatening.

5. **Confucian Dynamism** – in China and Japan, for example, where Confucian Dynamism is high, conformity according to position (obedience, deference) is valued. In the United States and Australia for example, where it is low, behaviour is less predictable.

Environmental analysis

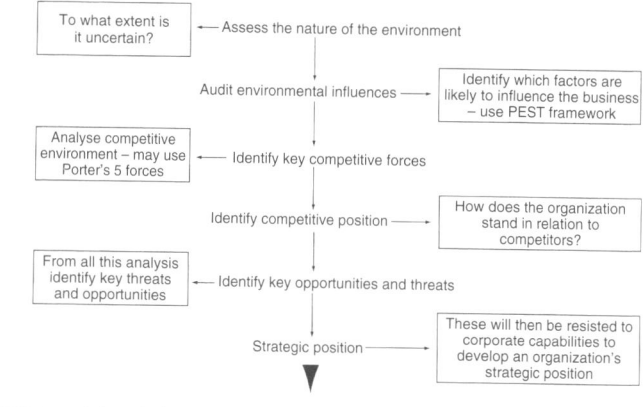

Fig. 2.1. Steps in environmental analysis
Source: Johnson and Scholes (1999)

Market sensing

Piercy (2002) suggests that the external environment should be monitored according to the probability of events and their impact on the organization.

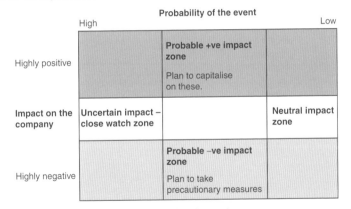

Fig. 2.2. An assessment framework for analysing the external environment

Organizational structure

Different environmental conditions require different organizational structures. Stacey suggests that:

■ Stable market environments are best served by mechanistic bureaucracies which deliver efficiency of operations.

■ Complex, rapidly changing environments are best served by organic forms.

■ Large organizations require divisional structures.

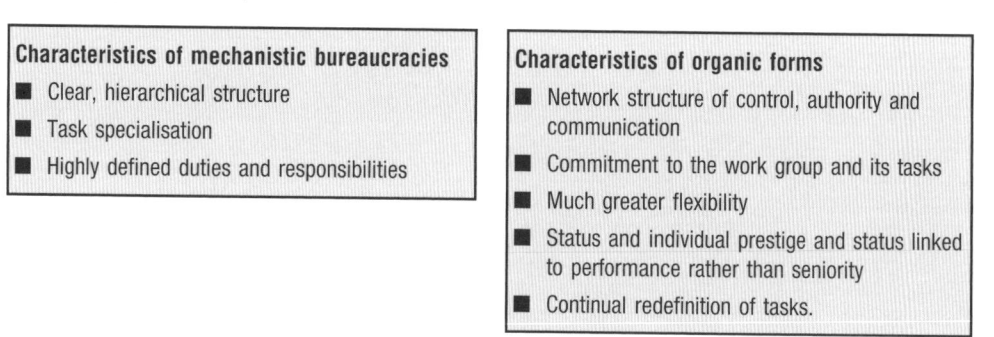

Characteristics of mechanistic bureaucracies

■ Clear, hierarchical structure

■ Task specialisation

■ Highly defined duties and responsibilities

Characteristics of organic forms

■ Network structure of control, authority and communication

■ Commitment to the work group and its tasks

■ Much greater flexibility

■ Status and individual prestige and status linked to performance rather than seniority

■ Continual redefinition of tasks.

Vision and values

Stakeholders influence an organization's vision and values to align with their own. Davidson (2002) suggests seven best practices in making Vision and Values work.

1. Define the organizational purpose and understand and link the needs of key stakeholders.
2. Establish a clear, distinctive vision that is customer related and is ambitious in terms of the organization's ability to achieve it.
3. Build strong values to support the vision based on key factors for success. It is essential that values are turned into measurable practices.
4. Communication is about leaders winning hearts and minds of senior managers who will then cascade this through the organization. This must ring true to the previous 'Best Practices'. For example, stating values as 'highest quality' or as 'teamwork' will not be embraced where people in the organization know and see 'average quality' as the accepted standard and a culture of 'blame' to be pervasive.
5. Organizational structure should facilitate vision and values and the latter should influence recruitment, training, reward and promotion, if this is to become 'embedded' in the organization.
6. Link branding to vision and values and ensure this addresses the needs of all stakeholders.
7. Measure committed customers, motivated employees and satisfied finance providers as a means of assessing how effectively visions and values are implemented.

Key drivers of change

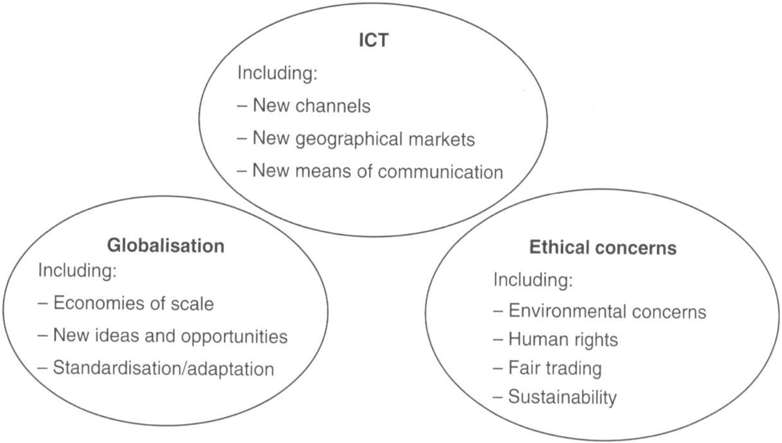

ICT
Including:
– New channels
– New geographical markets
– New means of communication

Globalisation
Including:
– Economies of scale
– New ideas and opportunities
– Standardisation/adaptation

Ethical concerns
Including:
– Environmental concerns
– Human rights
– Fair trading
– Sustainability

Revision tips

- The driving forces behind organizational culture are the various stakeholders, both internal and external.

- Frequently, the needs of these stakeholders have to be reconciled. The external environment, including external stakeholders, dictate what factors are critical to success in any market. An organization operating within that market must meet these critical success factors. Doing so may or may not be acceptable to the internal stakeholders.

- In the same way that there may be conflict between external and internal stakeholders, there may be conflicts within an organization.

- It is often these conflicts which give rise to the need for organizational change which is addressed in Unit 3.

- The assessment of the external environment may be achieved in a number of ways: traditional market research has now been widened to include all forms of knowledge management; econometric forecasting also has a place, as do more organic approaches such as market sensing. Ensure that you know the role that all of these can play in informing the development and implementation of an organization's strategy.

MANAGING CHANGE AND INTERNAL MARKETING

LEARNING OUTCOMES

9.63.2 Identify the barriers to effective implementation of strategies and plans involving change (including communications) in the organization, and develop measures to prevent or overcome them.

2.2. Assess the main pressures on an organization to change and the initiatives available or being used to respond.

2.3 Identify and evaluate the sources and the techniques for overcoming any resistance to change.

2.4 Assess the impact of, and prepare a plan for, change in a marketing department, including the development of appropriate skills and capabilities to meet the new objectives.

2.5 Critically evaluate the role and content of an internal marketing communications plan and its contribution to managing change in an organization.

Syllabus References: 9.63.2, 2.2–2.5

Planning and implementing change

■ In Unit 2 the drivers for change were examined. In this unit, the practicalities of implementing that change are addressed.

■ A range of theoretical approaches to change is available. Marketers manage change – in strategy, in positioning, in perception – on a frequent basis. As you revise this unit, consider how those theories apply to situations that you have encountered.

■ Internal marketing is an important technique in managing change. Again, think of the differing stakeholder groups in situations that you have encountered, the relative levels of interest and power of these

■ stakeholders, and how internal and external marketing may be used in different ways for each of them.

KEY DEFINITIONS

Planned approach to change – This approach views organizational change as essentially a process of moving from one fixed state to another through a series of predictable and pre-planned steps (Burnes, 1996).

Emergent approach to change – Starts from the assumption that change is a continuous, open-ended and unpredictable process of aligning and realigning an organization to its changing environment . . . views change as a process that unfolds through the interplay of multiple variables (context, political processes and consultation) within an organization (Burnes, 1996).

Project management – Involves achieving unity of purpose and setting achievable goals within given resources and timescales (Drummond and Ensor, 2001).

Internal marketing – This is a planned effort using a marketing-like approach directed at motivating employees, for implementing and integrating organizational strategies towards customer orientation (Ahmed and Rafiq, 2002).

Has the goal of developing a type of marketing programme aimed at the internal marketplace in the company that *parallels* and *matches* the marketing programme aimed at the external marketplace of customers and competitors (Piercy, 2002).

Internal relationship marketing – An integrative process within a system for fostering positive working relationship in a developmental way in a climate of co-operation and achievement. Varey and Lewis (1999), cited in Little and Marandi (2003).

Planning for change

The planned approach

Two main approaches to change are considered. Planned change is generally adopted within a stable predictable environment, whereas emergent change (considered on the next but one page) occurs more often in a turbulent or unpredictable environment.

The three-step model

Lewin (1958) suggests a broad approach consisting of three steps to achieve permanent change: -

1. Unfreezing the present level
2. Moving to the new level
3. Refreezing the new level

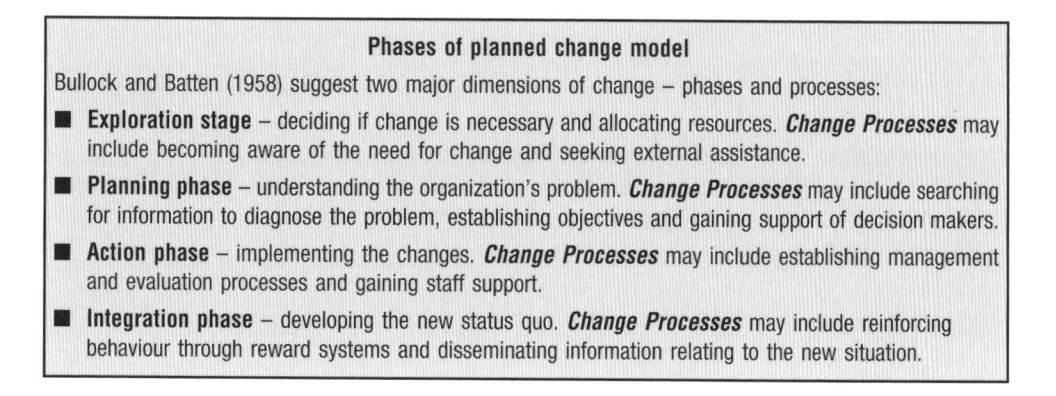

Phases of planned change model

Bullock and Batten (1958) suggest two major dimensions of change – phases and processes:

■ **Exploration stage** – deciding if change is necessary and allocating resources. *Change Processes* may include becoming aware of the need for change and seeking external assistance.

■ **Planning phase** – understanding the organization's problem. *Change Processes* may include searching for information to diagnose the problem, establishing objectives and gaining support of decision makers.

■ **Action phase** – implementing the changes. *Change Processes* may include establishing management and evaluation processes and gaining staff support.

■ **Integration phase** – developing the new status quo. *Change Processes* may include reinforcing behaviour through reward systems and disseminating information relating to the new situation.

Emergent change

Starts from the assumption that change is a continuous, open-ended and unpredictable process of aligning and realigning an organization to its changing environment... views change as a process that unfolds through the interplay of multiple variables (context, political processes and consultation) within an organization. (Burnes, 1996)

The main features of an emergent approach to change are as follows:

- Understanding the issues involved is viewed as more important than developing a detailed linear plan.
- It consists of a continuous process of experimentation and adaptation.
- Changes may be small-scale and incremental.
- The role of managers is to create a structure and climate which encourages change.

The change process

People

This is probably the most overlooked part of the change process. It involves the following:

Creating a willingness to change – It is essential that people are made aware of the need for change and that a positive attitude is created.

Involving people – Effective communication (two-way) can assist in achieving 'buy in' to the change process so that people will be involved and can take ownership of the process.

Sustaining the momentum – This can be helped by ensuring that sufficient resources are available, support, including training necessary to acquire new skills, is given to the 'change agents' and desired behaviour is reinforced through rewards.

Burnes (1996) suggests that, following the setting of objectives, planning the change should involve six activities:

1. Establishing a change management team
2. Management structures
3. Activity planning
4. Commitment planning
5. Audit and post-audit
6. Training

Adapting to change

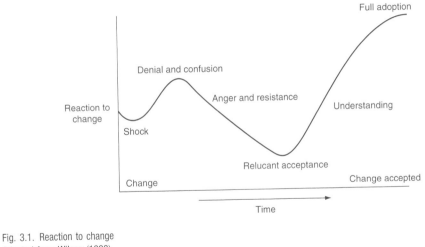

Fig. 3.1. Reaction to change
Adapted from Wilson (1993)

Successful implementation

Bonoma (1984) suggests that various combinations of a strategy and an organization's ability to implement that strategy lead to different business outcomes.

Success – when an effective strategy is implemented well.

Chance – when the strategy itself is weak but it is well implemented. In this case there is a chance of success.

Problem – A strong strategy is poorly executed, resulting in problems.

Failure – This is very likely to occur when an inappropriate strategy is poorly implemented.

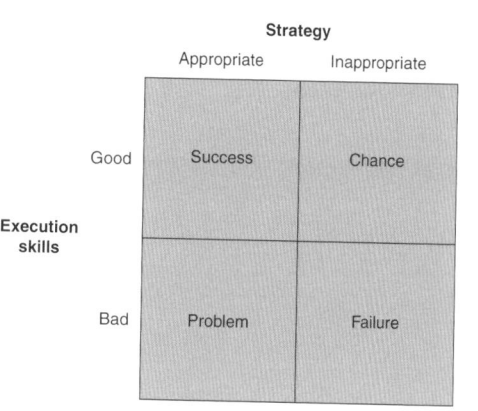

Fig. 3.2. Strategy and execution

Factors in a successful implementation

Table 3.1.

Factor	Comment
Leadership	A strong and effective leader that is able to motivate and build teams is an essential ingredient for successful implementation.
Culture	Culture refers to the shared values and beliefs. If a plan goes against the dominant culture, it is likely the plan will fail, unless support is gained via internal marketing.
Structure	Organizational structures not only denote levels of responsibility but also facilitate communication. Communication is a key aspect of implementation and organizations must ensure that the structures do not act as barriers to effective communication.
Resources	Appropriate levels of resources should be available – time, money and staff.
Control	Effective controls should be established to measure the progress and success of plans.
Skills	Skills necessary for successful implementation include technical/marketing skills, HRM skills and project management skills.
Strategy	An appropriate and relevant strategy must be communicated to all participants.
Systems	Effective systems should be in place, for example, marketing information systems that generate relevant and timely information.

Adapted from Drummond and Ensor (2001)

McKinsey 7-S framework

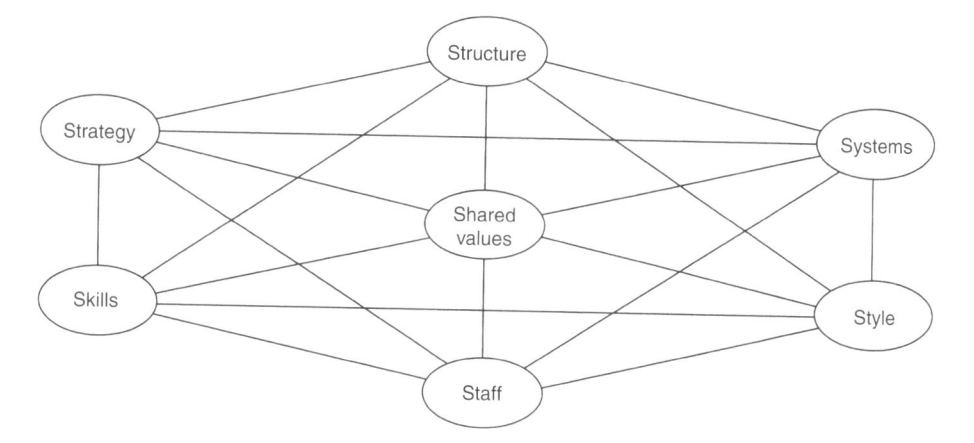

Fig. 3.3. Mckinsey 7-S framework
Adapted from Drummond and Ensor (2001)

Project management

Table 3.2. Common tasks in project management

Task	Comment
Objective setting	It is important that objectives are SMART (Specific, Measurable, Action, Realistic and Timebound).
Planning	This involves breaking down the project into manageable tasks, co-ordinating activities and monitoring progress.
Delegation	The key to successful management is the recognition that you cannot do everything yourself.
Team building	An essential skill for a project manager is the ability to build a successful team.
Crisis management	There will be times when things do not go according to plan and urgent action is required. In order to try to anticipate likely problems, scenario planning can be used.

Adapted from Drummond and Ensor (2001)

Internal marketing
Three types of marketing

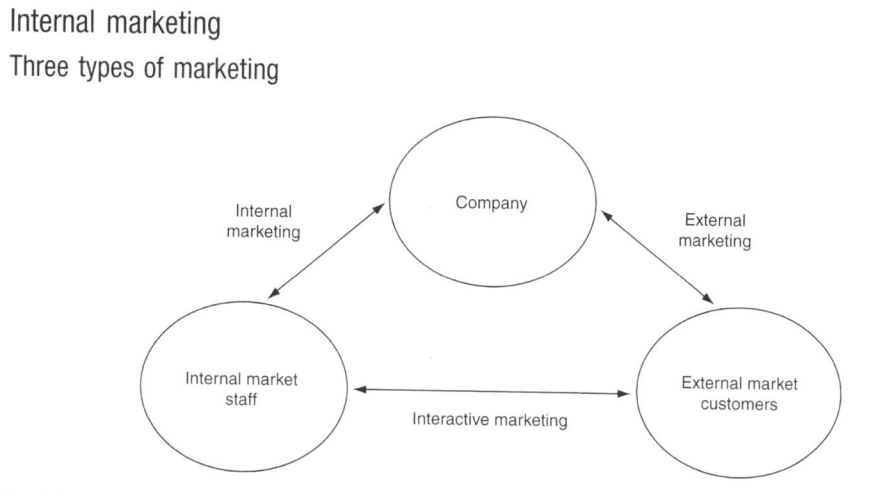

Fig. 3.4.
Adapted from Kotler *et al.* (1999)

Internal marketing

Ahmed and Rafiq (2002) define internal marketing as follows and go on to identify five main elements:

Internal marketing is a planned effort using a marketing-like approach directed at motivating employees, for implementing and integrating organizational strategies towards customer orientation.

1. **Employee motivation and satisfaction** – IM acts as a vehicle for staff acquisition, motivation and retention that in turn leads to increased productivity and external service quality.

2. **Customer orientation and customer satisfaction** – IM can promote customer-orientated behaviour among staff.

3. **Inter-functional co-ordination and integration** – these are key elements of a market orientation as identified by Narver and Slater (1999). IM can be used to co-ordinate the efforts of the different functions in an organization.

4. **Marketing-like approach** to the above – other tools can be used to achieve the above. However, IM relies on achieving these through the use of marketing principles and tools.

5. **Implementation of specific corporate or functional strategies** – Piercy (2002) suggests that IM plays a crucial role in the implementation of strategic change by ensuring understanding and support for the strategies and also for removing barriers to change.

The internal marketing plan

This has the same format as an external marketing plan, with objectives, strategy, market segmentation, marketing mix programme and evaluation and control. A number of aspects are worthy of note.

Internal market segmentation

Internal markets may be segmented in a number of ways, including location or job function. A number of writers suggest the following:

- Supporters
- Neutrals
- Opposers

The internal marketing mix

This should encompass the same elements as the External Marketing Mix – Product, Place, Price, Promotion, Physical Evidence and Process.

Internal marketing execution

Successful execution of the internal plan is reliant on three key skills (Jobber, 2001, p. 658):

1. Persuasion – the ability to develop a persuasive argument and to support words with action.
2. Negotiation – it is likely that some negotiations will have to take place so that all parties are happy.
3. Politics – organizations are made up of people, all with their own personal agendas. Therefore, it is essential that the sources of power are identified and used to help implement the plan.

Internal marketing and relationship marketing

Transaction-based internal marketing

One-way internal communication used to inform staff. Job design and development are viewed as the internal product and the price being the salary and training costs.

Some attempts at two-way communication between staff and organization. Management continues to make major decisions about strategy, albeit after considering staff views.

Relationship-based internal marketing

Two-way dialogue between management and staff. Role of senior managers is one of facilitator rather than leader or decision maker. The strategic direction of the company is developed jointly from the experiences and knowledge of staff and customers.

Fig. 3.5. Continuum of internal relationship marketing
Adapted from Little and Marandi (2003)

Revision tips

■ Change may be achieved in different ways according to the organizational context. Whilst achieving change through an emergent rather than a planned approach may appear easier, in fact, for an emergent approach to be effective, the right organizational context must be created, which represents a significant task in itself.

■ Consider both the different approaches to the processes involved in change and the way in which those processes may be phased in order to achieve sustained change.

■ The skills and resources available are also important factors in successfully completing a change programme. Consider particularly the soft skills, using a model such as the 7-S framework, to assess an organization's current and required positions.

■ Internal marketing is an important technique in bringing about change. Although the structure is the same as that of an external marketing plan, there is plenty of scope to demonstrate your knowledge and understanding.

■ Crucially, do not neglect the practicalities and realities. Political activity is important. Think through how this might best be carried out. For a large company, a formal change programme may be appropriate: for a smaller organization, such as BCCL from the December 2005 paper, a far less formal approach is required – what price walking around engaging with internal stakeholders over a cup of coffee?

IMPLEMENTING THE BUSINESS STRATEGY THROUGH MARKETING ACTIVITIES

LEARNING OUTCOMES

9.63.2 Identify the barriers to effective implementation of strategies and plans involving change (including communications) in the organization, and develop measures to prevent or overcome them.

9.63.5 Initiate and critically evaluate systems for control of marketing activities undertaken as part of business and marketing plans.

3.1 Explain the link between marketing activities and shareholder value, and measurement using economic value added.

3.2 Determine the contribution to shareholder value of marketing activities undertaken.

3.3 Build sustainability and ethics into business and marketing activities (including the mix) through planning, the instillation of values and day-to-day management.

Syllabus References: 9.63.2, 9.63.5, 3.1–3.3

The strategic marketing manager's role

This unit focuses on the developing role of Marketing as it has moved through its lifecycle. The focus has moved away from transactions and now relationships are very much to the fore. These must, however, be seen to deliver value to shareholders and the ways in which this can be demonstrated are examined in this unit.

An important stakeholder for most organizations is the community or communities in which they operate. The role of, and justification for, corporate social responsibility is also considered here as an important element or Marketing's remit.

The underlying theme here is that the greater part of the value of most organizations lies in their intangible assets, including reputation, brands, the customer base and knowledge of the marketplace. The investment in many of these is controlled by the Marketing Managers of the organization, who are responsible, therefore, for adding value to the organization by managing these assets and relationships.

KEY DEFINITIONS

Value added – the difference between the (comprehensively accounted) value of the firm's outputs and the (comprehensively accounted) cost of firm's inputs (Kay, 2003).

Shareholder value add – the discounted value of future cash flows over time (after Doyle, 2000).

Discounted cash flow – future cash flows multiplied by the discount factor to obtain the present value of the cash flows (Doyle, 2000).

Net present value – a net contribution of a strategy to the wealthy shareholders: present value of cash flows – initial investment (Doyle, 2000).

Corporate social responsibility – the social responsibility of business encompasses the economic, legal, ethical and discretionary (philanthropic) expectations that society has of organizations at a given point in time (Carroll and Buchholtz, 2003).

Ethics – a set of moral principles or values that deal with what is good and bad with respect to moral duty and obligation (after Carroll and Buchholtz, 2003).

Business ethics – is concerned with i.e., 'right' and 'wrong' behaviours and practices that take place with a business context. Often interpreted to include questions of fairness, justice and equity (after Carroll and Buchholtz, 2003).

The marketing manager's role

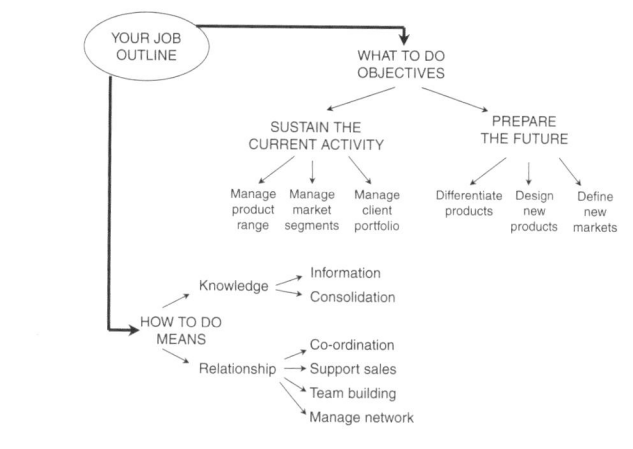

Fig 4.1. The marketer's role
Adapted from Millier and Palmer (2000)

Context map

		Market orientation	
		Low	High
Your relative marketing expertise	High	*Steer & give direction*	*Sustain & develop*
	Low	*Understand & define*	*Learn & develop*

Fig. 4.2. Context map
Source: Adapted from Millier and Palmer (2000)

The life cycle of marketing

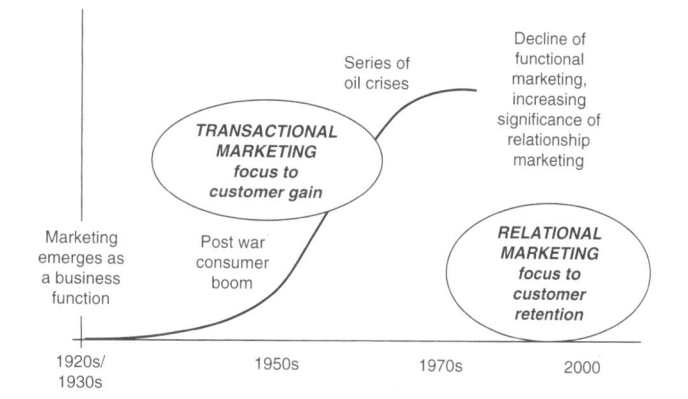

Fig. 4.3. The life cycle of marketing
Adapted from Brookes and Palmer (2004)

Implications of relationship marketing

Gronroos (1990) defines Relationship Marketing as follows:

The role of relationship marketing is to identify, establish, maintain and enhance relationships with customers and other stakeholders, at a profit, so that the objectives of all other parties involved are met; and that this is done by a mutual exchange and fulfillment of promises.

Brookes and Palmer (2004) concluded that there were five major drivers for change in the nature of relationship marketing practices. These lead to the implications for marketing practice set out on the following page:

1. The requirement for increased financial accountability, and focus to loyalty and customer value management

2. The increasing emphasis on service aspects of all products

3. Organizational transformation to reduce costs and increase service

4. Increasing retailer power and the role of systemic relationships within networks

5. The rise of interactive media, the need for mass customisation.

Implications of relationship marketing

Table 4.1. Implications for marketing practice

Business environment	Customer
Increasingly global nature of competition	More sophisticated
More demanding legislative requirements	Lower brand preference
Increasing social awareness	Market saturation
	Inelastic demand
	Increased price sensitivity
Industry	**Company**
Technology maturity	Potential to maintain return on investment
Overcapacity	Limited resources
Stabilisation of production methods	Little opportunity for differentiation
Technology and cumulative experience common	Increase in private label
Stabilisation and concentration of market shares	Product modification rather than innovation

Adapted from Brookes and Palmer (2004)

Multiple markets model

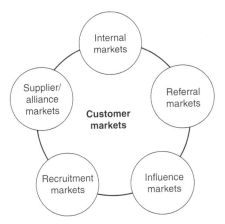

Fig. 4.4.
Source: Christopher, Payne and Ballantyne (1991)

Accounting systems and value added

One of the main objectives of business is to maximise shareholders wealth by adding value to the company or organization. Three methods of measuring this Shareholder Added Value are considered.

Cashflow valuation

The calculation of cashflow generated by a strategy can be split into two parts: -

1. Present Value (PV) of Cashflow during the forecast period. Calculated as the PV of the net cashflows (income less expenditure) during the forecast period.

2. PV of Cashflow after the period (residual value)

The latter is difficult to attribute to marketing strategies and so they may be evaluated on the basis of the first alone.

Economic value added

This is simply the amount by which the return on an investment exceeds the cost of the capital required for that investment.

EVA = Net Operating Profits After Tax
    − (capital invested × weighted average cost of that capital)

The figure in brackets is effectively the return that could have been secured by investing that capital elsewhere.

Return on Capital Employed (ROCE)

$$ROCE = \frac{\text{Earnings Before Interest \& Tax} * 100\%}{\text{Capital Employed}}$$

Doyle is critical of this measure because the value of earnings (which includes the value of assets) may be arbitrary and subject to risk.

Developing shareholder value

Peterson (2004) suggests that there are six **sources or drivers of added value**:

1. **Economies of scale** – as output increases this introduces efficiencies in production and also learning effects whereby better techniques and processes are developed.

2. **Economies of scope** – this is where an investment, such as a research laboratory, for example, can support not just the original activity but others in addition.

3. **Cost advantages** – sometimes known as first-mover advantages, where those who are first into a market have the opportunity to build brands and relationships, gain best access to distribution channels and so on and hence increase the cost to others who wish to enter the market and compete.

4. **Product differentiation** – the more effectively a product can be differentiated, perhaps by the use of patents or brand name, the greater the opportunity to increase revenue and sustain margins.

5. **Access to distribution channel** – when product differentiation diminishes, particularly in mature markets, then access to and control of distribution channels is an effective form of competition.

6. **Government policy** – changes or increases in regulation can affect the perceived attractiveness of a market and may act to reduce the number of competitors.

The Boston matrix

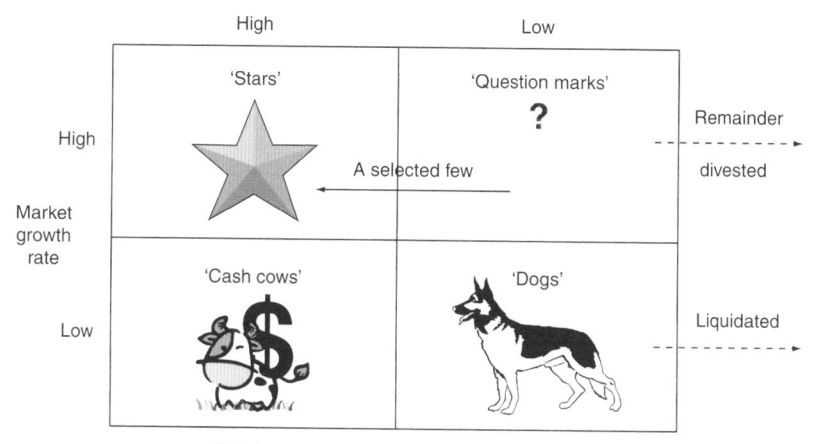

Fig. 4.5. The Boston matrix and shareholder value

Corporate social responsibility

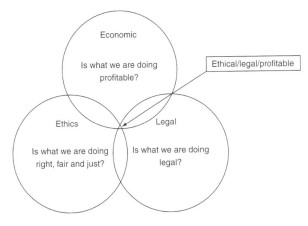

Fig. 4.6. Ethical management
Adapted from Carroll and Buchholtz (2003)

The increasing importance of corporate social responsibility

The reasons that Corporate Social Responsibility has become so important can be summarized as:

Technology – information and communications technology has developed exponentially in recent years. This has given individuals unprecedented access to information by means of the Internet. There is a much higher degree of visibility and exposure of business actions.

Globalisation – the rise of technology, the lower cost of international communications, travel and trade and changes in the world order has seen globalisation and develop significantly. Brands are now truly global in their reach and manufacturing is moving from high wage, Western economies to lower-cost Pacific Rim countries and China.

Affluence and Education – has led to a society that is much more questioning of business and demanding of rights with clearly communicated expectations. Pressure groups now have the power to confront the largest companies in the world and the purchasing power of individuals can be used to directly influence companies alongside other forms of direct and indirect action.

Rights and Entitlement – there is now an increasing trend for society to be aware of its rights, with numerous pressure groups representing increasingly fragmented groups. Each of these groups consider that they have an entitlement to certain privileges. At the same time it has been suggested that those who do not receive their anticipated entitlements are therefore victims.

Arguments for and against adopting corporate social responsibility

Table 4.2. CSR – A cause for concern and action?

Why not CSR?	Why CSR?
The purpose for a business is to reward shareholders and not to be involved in wider social issues	Wider social issues in society exist because of the existence of businesses, which have a responsibility to assist in addressing them
Business is not the appropriate vehicle with which to address the wider issues in society	Business is a part of society and it is in the long-term interest of the business to be socially responsible
Engaging in wider issues takes managers away from the primary purpose of business	By not being seen to act responsibly, society will impose constraints on business by means of regulation and other actions
Business already has significant power and influence in society and should not be allowed more	Business employs skilled and capable people who have the capability to address wider social issues
By becoming involved in wider social issues, the business takes on costs which should be borne elsewhere and is therefore disadvantaged relative to competitors	By anticipating and managing potential social issues, this is a cheaper and more effective way of dealing with them
Managers are employed because of their functional skills and are not primarily suited to engagement in wider social issues	All stakeholders, including business, take responsibility to at least try to address social issues

Adapted from Carroll and Buchholtz (2003)

Revision tips

■ The focus of this unit is on how the Marketing professional can add value to an organization and, equally importantly, demonstrate that value has been added. Ensure, therefore, that you understand the concept of value and the techniques for measuring it.

■ Relationships have a crucial role to play in adding value to all organizations. An important step in developing these relationships is the identification and classification of stakeholders and stakeholder groups. This is a recurring theme in this examination.

■ Key stakeholders will include the community and society at large. Corporate Social Responsibility (CSR) is a topical issue for Marketers. In addition to making sure that you are familiar with its treatment in the set texts, examine examples of the way that organizations use it to position themselves to their stakeholders. Take a look, for example, at the websites for companies with challenging issues to resolve, such as British American Tobacco (www.bat.com), to see how they address such issues.

■ The relationship between CSR, reputation and branding, leading to the generation of shareholder value through investing in increasing the value of intangible assets is a constant theme of this module. Ensure that you understand this by addressing Question 4 of the December 2005 Paper.

IMPLEMENTING THE BUSINESS STRATEGY THROUGH MARKETING ACTIVITIES

LEARNING OUTCOMES

9.63.3 Demonstrate an ability to manage marketing activities as part of strategic implementation.

9.63.4 Assess an organization's needs for marketing skills and resources and develop strategies for acquiring, developing and retaining them.

3.4 Critically appraise methods available for valuing brands and building brand equity, and recommend an appropriate approach for the organization.

3.5 Propose a contingency plan and procedures to be taken in the event of a 'crisis' or threat to the reputation of the brand or the organization (including communications with the press and stakeholders).

LEARNING OUTCOMES – CONTINUED

3.6   Identify 'moments of truth' in delivering a service and activities that may add further value, and assess their likely impact on customers and intermediaries.

3.8   Establish and apply techniques for managing and monitoring service quality, including the use of specific measures.

Syllabus References: 9.63.3, 9.63.4, 3.4–3.8

Marketing actions to enhance reputation – 1

This unit builds on the concepts developed in Unit 4 and examines practical ways in which they, and other marketing principles, can add value to an organization, principally by enhancing its reputation. The focus, therefore, is on:

■ The drivers of value – intangibles such as brands and reputation.

■ The ways in which these drivers can be evaluated.

■ The development of processes to maintain and enhance this value.

The emphasis in this unit is on building value on the basis of enhancing the organization's reputation and so brand value. The management of service quality and identification of 'moments of truth' will achieve this objective. However, it is also necessary to put in place plans to safeguard those assets should there be any threat to them. So crisis management and contingency planning are considered.

Note also the links to change management. Whilst the process of change is carried out, it is important to maintain the levels of customer service and take action should the organization's reputation be threatened.

KEY DEFINITIONS

Brand equity – a set of assets and liabilities linked to a brand's name and symbol that add to or subtract from the value provided by a product or service to a firm and/or that firm's customers (Aaker, 1998, p. 173).

Contingency planning – the advance preparation of a course of action to meet events that are not expected, but will have a significant impact on the organization if they occur (O'Connor, 1978).

Service encounter – service encounters take place whenever customers, whether end consumers or intermediaries, come in contact (or interact) with the organization or its people.

Service quality – the consumer's overall impression of the relative inferiority/superiority of the organization and its services (Bitner and Hubbert, 1994, p. 77).

Service quality is when service delivery (i.e. the perceived service) meets or exceeds customer's expectations.

Brand valuation

The value of brands, as intangible assets, is not usually shown on a company's balance sheet. The exception occurs when one company acquires another at a price in excess of its book value. In that case, the value of the intangible assets acquired which justified the premium over the book value will be shown on the acquiring company's balance sheet, usually under the heading of 'Goodwill'.

Partly in order to justify investment in brands, however, it is useful to establish a method of valuing brands and so any increase in value due to investment in them. The Brand Value Chain, shown on the next page, illustrates how brands, and investment in them, can deliver shareholder value. There are also other conceptual models shown on the next page but one. A number of methodologies are proposed to try to quantify the extent to which brands can add value to an organization:

■ Stockmarket-based. This is a simplistic approach which is based on measures including historical investment in advertising and the age of the brand.

■ Value-added approaches are based on the additional revenue that a brand can generate through, for example, premium pricing. Little attention, however, is paid to the increase in value of the brand.

■ The Economic Use Method uses broader measures, looking at the Net Present Value of a range of contributions to the business.

■ Finally, Interbrand's approach is based on an economic model that includes direct and future earnings and also the vulnerability of the brand to risk.

Brand value chain

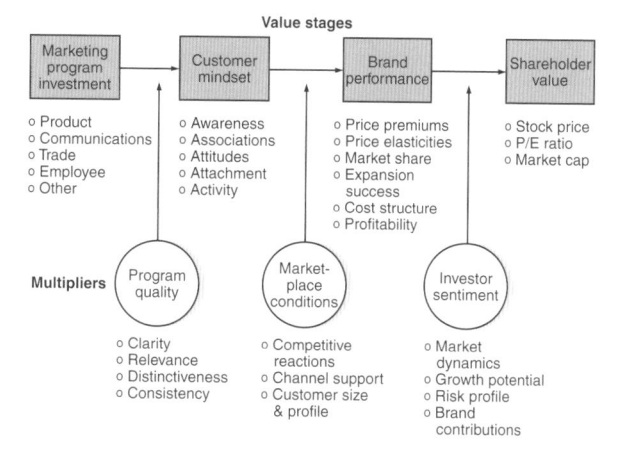

Fig. 5.1.
Source: Keller and Lehmann (2003)

Brand Equity Models

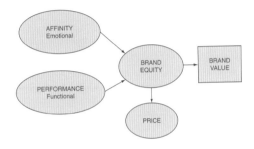

Fig. 5.2. RI brand equity engine

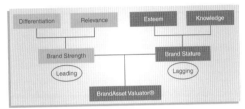

Fig. 5.3. Y&R's BrandAsset Valuator

Contingency and crisis planning

Crises can occur in many forms, discrete or continuous, and represent a considerable risk to an organization's reputation and so to shareholder value. Effective crisis management is founded on identification of key stakeholders, particularly the media, and sound prior contingency planning.

> *Crisis Management* is a mindset and process that, on a daily basis, drives an organization's decisions and actions... the goal of crisis management is to help organizations avert crises or more effectively manage those that do occur.
>
> (Pearson *et al.*, 1997)

> *A Crisis* is an event, revelation, allegation or set of circumstances which threatens the integrity, reputation, or survival of an individual or organization. It challenges the public's sense of safety, values or appropriateness. The actual or potential damage to the organization is considerable.

> *Contingency Planning* is the advance preparation of a course of action to meet events that are not expected, but will have a significant impact on the organization if they occur.
>
> (O'Connor, 1978)

The crisis lifecycle

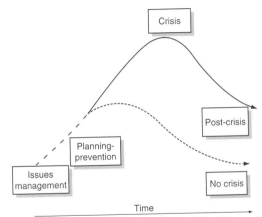

Fig. 5.4.
Source: Gonzales-Herrero and Pratt (1996)

Crisis management

Pearson *et al.* (1997) identify five phases of Crisis Management

1. **Signal detection** – looking for warning signals – 'in the best prepared organizations, detecting signals is not left to chance'.
2. **Preparation** – when organizations do what they can to avoid crises, and manage those that occur.
3. **Damage Containment** – Fortune 100 companies spend most crisis management resources to this phase, which attempts to limit the spread of the crisis damage. This should be prepared in advance as the costs of providing this service are high, and the processes are difficult.
4. **Recovery** – focuses on short- and long-term plans for the organization.
5. **Learning** – this is when the organization reviews what has happened to ensure better practice in the future. Often organizations want to forget the crisis, and so fail to learn.

Service quality – ServQual dimensions

It is very important to understand that service quality represents the *customer's* perception of the level of service delivery relative to expectations. This can be measured on the dimensions shown below. The *underlying drivers* of that service delivery are internal to the organization and are analysed using the Gaps model shown on page 77.

Table 5.1. ServQual dimensions

ServQual dimension	Description
Reliability	Ability to perform the promised service dependably and accurately
Responsiveness	Willingness to help customers and provide prompt service
Assurance	Employees' knowledge and courtesy and their ability to inspire trust and confidence
Empathy	Caring, individualised attention given to customers
Tangibles	Appearance of physical facilities, equipment, personnel and written materials

Source: Zeithaml and Bitner (2003)

Service quality

Customer perceptions of quality and customer satisfaction

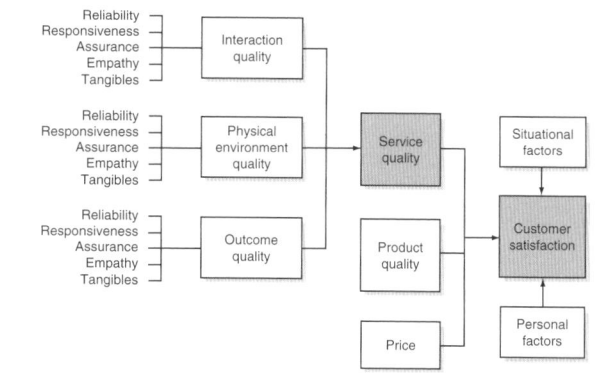

Fig. 5.5. Customer perceptions of quality and customer satisfaction
Source: Zeithaml and Bitner (2003)

Service interactions

Shostack (1985) identifies three types of service encounters:

Remote encounters – customer contact with the organization is through impersonal means. Nowadays, this is usually through some form of computer interaction, such as people banking through ATMs and websites.

Phone encounters – whether for enquiries, orders, service delivery and customer service.

Face-to-face encounters – direct personal contacts between the customers and employees for any purpose, for example part of the sales process or the service delivery process.

Creating measurable service encounters

Zeithaml and Bitner (2003) present four key themes:

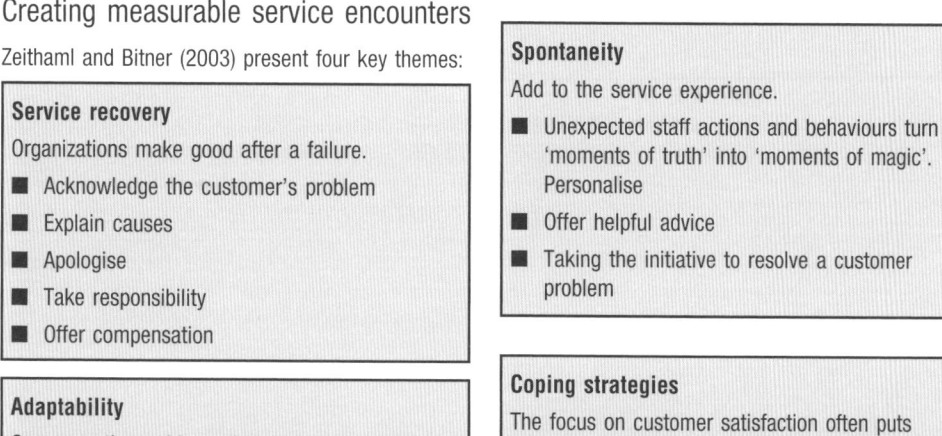

Service recovery

Organizations make good after a failure.

- Acknowledge the customer's problem
- Explain causes
- Apologise
- Take responsibility
- Offer compensation

Adaptability

Overcome the problems that customers believe stem from the organization's systems.

- Recognise/acknowledge customers' needs
- Explain why the systems are required.

Spontaneity

Add to the service experience.

- Unexpected staff actions and behaviours turn 'moments of truth' into 'moments of magic'. Personalise
- Offer helpful advice
- Taking the initiative to resolve a customer problem

Coping strategies

The focus on customer satisfaction often puts employees under pressure to resolve problems.

- Empower employees to make decisions and deal with conflict to avoid the situation escalating.

ServQual gaps model

This model allows Service Quality to be defined as the Customer Gap – The Gap between Perceived and Expected Service. This Gap may then be broken down into Gaps 1–4 to allow causes to be identified and addressed.

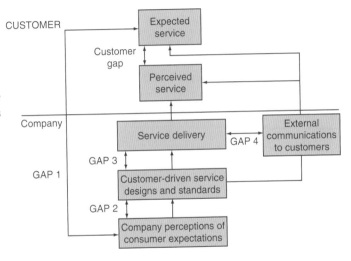

Fig. 5.6.
Source: Zeithaml and Bitner (2003)

Service balanced scorecard

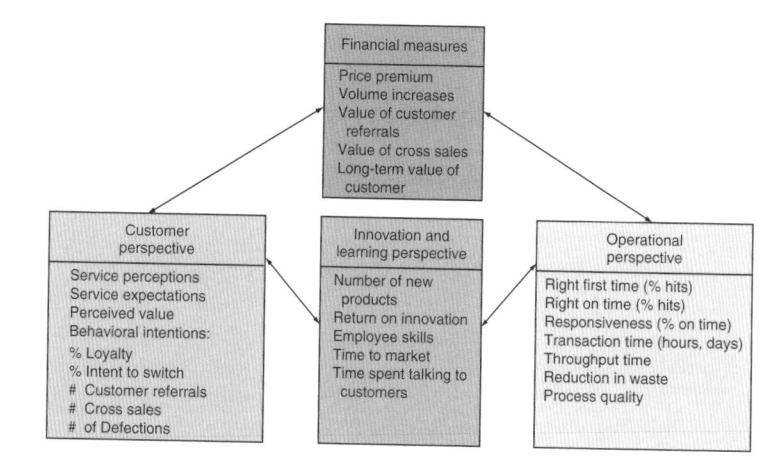

Fig. 5.7.
Source: Zeithaml and Bitner (2003)

Revision tips

■ The focus of this unit is on maintaining and enhancing an organization's reputation.

■ Ensure that you are familiar with the intangible factors that contribute to that reputation which include brands and service quality.

■ Consider the ways in which these can be measured and assessed (brand valuation and service quality) and apply the tools that enable this to be achieved (Brand valuation tools and ServQual dimensions and gaps model).

■ The ServQual Gaps model and the five dimensions of service quality are widely applicable and you should ensure that you are familiar with them.

■ This application enables processes to be established, such as contingency planning and customer service processes.

■ Very often, models such as ServQual enable business issues within an organization, which have an effect on customers. to be identified clearly, thereby indicating how customer service can be safeguarded. For example, should an organization be considering recruitment, it is important to identify the roles required. If understanding customer needs is an issue (ServQual Gap 1), then a researcher may be recruited. If, however, the service is designed correctly but delivery is an issue (ServQual Gap 3), an Operations Manager may be the right solution. See December 2006 paper, Question 1a.

IMPLEMENTING THE BUSINESS STRATEGY THROUGH MARKETING ACTIVITIES

Unit 6

LEARNING OUTCOMES

9.63.3 Demonstrate and ability to manage marketing activities as part of strategic implementation.

9.63.4 Assess an organization's needs for marketing skills and resources and develop strategies for acquiring, developing and retaining them.

3.7 Propose and implement appropriate improvements to customer service by developing or enhancing customer care programmes.

3.9 Develop and manage integrated marketing and communications programmes to establish and build relationships appropriate to the needs of customers, clients or intermediaries.

3.10 Develop support for relationships with customers, clients and intermediaries using appropriate information systems and databases and adhering to relevant privacy and data protection legislation.

Syllabus References: 9.63.3, 9.63.4, 3.7, 3.9, 3.10

Marketing action to enhance reputation – 2

This unit follows on from Unit 5 in building on the concepts developed in Unit 4 and examining practical ways in which they, and other marketing principles, can add value to an organization by enhancing its reputation. The focus, in this case, is on:

■ The practicalities of customer care programmes and processes.

■ The use of integrated marketing communications in establishing and building relationships with stakeholders.

■ The use of information systems and databases to support these relationships and the importance of adhering to relevant privacy and data protection legislation.

KEY DEFINITIONS

Customer service – Customer service is a supplementary service to any organization's core offering (Parasuraman, 1998).

The activities that support orders, including application, advice, configuration, order processing, handling, post-sale communication and special services. The primary objective of customer service is to increase customer satisfaction, operational efficiency and customer loyalty. www.fivetwelve group.com/question.html.

Integrated marketing communications (IMC) programmes – An integrated marketing communication program requires that: (1) multiple types of communication options are employed and (2) communication options are designed in a way to reflect the existence and content of other communication options in the program (Keller, 2001, p. 822).

Customer relationship management (CRM) – A comprehensive strategy and process of acquiring, retaining, and partnering with selective customers to create superior value for the company and the customer. It involves the integration of marketing, sales, customer service, and the supply-chain functions of the organization to achieve greater efficiencies and effectiveness in delivering customer value (Parvatiyar and Sheth, 2001). **A technology – enabled implementation of the marketing concept**.

Customer service

Customer service is an important means of differentiating companies operating in the same market. It is also a driver of customer retention and so profitability.

A Mintel report comments:

The value in using service to differentiate an offer is that it can be harder to negate by a competitor. Unlike price-matching, which negates a competitor's price advantage, service provision reflects a company's 'personality' and enhances a retailer's brand value.

Fig. 6.1. The relationship marketing orientation
Source: Christopher, Payne and Ballantyne (2002)

Roles of customer service

Table 6.1. Customer service components at different stages in product purchase and use

Pre-transaction	Pre-contact	Advertising
		Technical information
		Written policies
		System flexibility
Transaction	Personal contact	Sales call
		Presentation/demonstration
	Pre-delivery	Order placement
		Document processing
		Inventory policy
		Order assembly
Post-transaction	Delivery	Transportation
		Receiving
		Installation
	Post-delivery	Product performance
		Product support
		Implementation
		Training

Source: Christopher (1992)

Integrated marketing communications

Integration of marketing communications is achieved at a number of levels:

Integration of the promotional activity with the overall marketing programmes. Promotion should, therefore, be consistent with the company objectives and strategy, as well as the marketing objectives and strategy.

Integration of each of the aspects of the marketing and promotional activity with each other. Logos, branding, corporate colours and standards should be consistent across the company.

Choice of media to produce integrated campaigns. Media used should complement each other to deliver differentiation, reinforcement, information or persuasion as appropriate.

Integration of brand strategies and promotional delivery in different markets. The standardisation/adaptation decision is often complex. The objective, however is to achieve a balance between the power and effectiveness of a global brand and the appeal to the specific needs of individual markets.

Integrated Marketing Communications for trade and consumer channels. Consumer campaigns can be leveraged in establishing relationships with trade customers as they generate consumer 'pull' and so make the subject of the campaign more attractive to the trade channels.

Integrated marketing communications

Keller (2001) identifies six criteria that impact on the effectiveness and efficiency of a communications programme

1. Coverage – the proportion of target customers reached by each marketing communications option.

2. Contribution – the ability of a form of marketing communication to create the desired response in isolation of any other form of communication.

3. Commonality – the common associations that exist and are reinforced in communication options, that is, the extent to which meaning is shared in different marketing communications.

4. Complementarity – the extent to which communications options can show, emphasise or develop different associations.

5. Robustness – the extent to which forms of marketing communication are effective for different consumers, bearing in mind the different levels of prior experience and exposure.

6. Cost – these criteria should be considered in the context of cost to determine their value in an Integrated Marketing Communications Programme.

Establishing relationships

Organizations increase the value of their customers by moving them up the Ladder of Loyalty:

Partner – someone who has the relationship of a partner with you

Advocate – someone who actively recommends you to others

Supporter – someone who likes your organization, but supports you only passively

Client – someone who has done business with you on a repeat basis but may be negative, or at best neutral, towards your organization

Customer – someone who has done business just once with your organization

Prospect – someone whom you believe may do business with you.

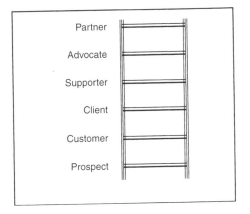

Fig. 6.2. The ladder of loyalty
Source: Peck, Payne Christopher and Clark (1999)

Customer relationship management

McCorkell (1999) identifies that direct and database marketing is built on four dimensions:

1. **Targeting** – who are the targets for the offer?
2. **Interaction** – how can we communicate and what should we communicate?
3. **Control** – what is the return on the investment?
4. **Continuity** – how can we build the relationship?

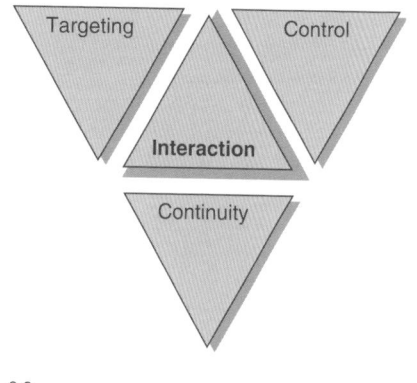

Fig. 6.3.
Source: McCorkell (1999)

Relationship management

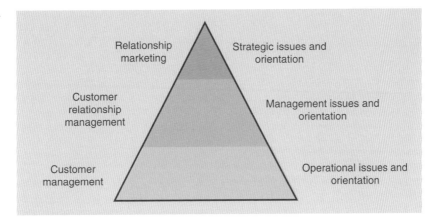

Fig. 6.4. Relationship management at strategic, tactical and operational levels
Source: Payne (2004)

CRM strategy

The CRM strategy framework

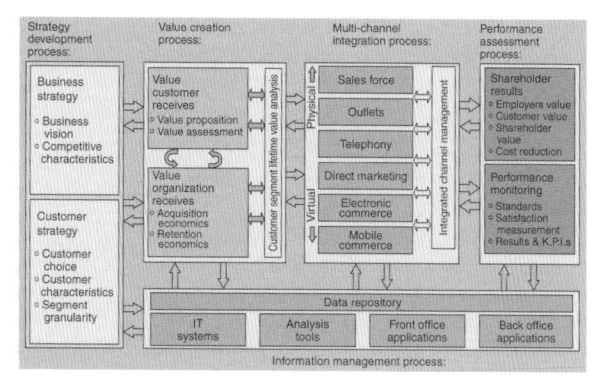

Fig. 6.5. The CRM strategy framework
Source: Payne (2004)

Data protection

Table 6.2. Principles of data protection in Europe

1. Data should be processed fairly and lawfully.
2. Data should be processed for limited purposes and not in any way that is incompatible with these purposes.
3. Data is adequate, relevant and not excessive.
4. Data is accurate.
5. Data is kept only as long as necessary.
6. Data is processed in line with individual's rights.
7. Data is kept secure.
8. Data is not transferred to other countries that cannot provide adequate data protection.

Source: Business Link (2004)

Customers have certain rights with regard to information held about them. These include: The right of access, such as to see information held on them.

- The right to prevent processing of data that can cause distress, such as revealing financial information to a third party without consent.

- The right to prevent processing for direct marketing, such as preventing organizations from using data for direct-marketing purposes.

- The right to compensation for damage or distress resulting from inappropriate use of personal data, where the Data Controller cannot show reasonable care in complying with the Act.

- The right to have data rectified, blocked, erased or destroyed.

- The right to prevent an organization from selling or passing on information without permission.

- The right to have personal data kept secure from unauthorised access.

- The right not to have data that is important deleted from an organization's records.

Revision tips

■ Like Unit 5, the focus of this unit is again on maintaining and enhancing an organization's reputation, in this case the focus being on the more practical aspects that lead to a higher degree of customer loyalty.

■ Ensure that you are familiar with the criteria for good customer service and the processes that deliver this service.

■ A broad understanding of all aspects of integrated marketing communications is essential at this level and it is wise to read widely on this subject.

■ Whilst CRM is often construed as simply an IT system, it is a far broader subject, which covers criteria for the segmentation of customers and consequent allocation of resources in order to both deliver an appropriate level of value to those customers and secure a maximum level of value from them. It is essential to understand how this is achieved.

■ Finally, it is important to know the legal and ethical constraints on using personal data. In particular, a broad understanding of the principles of the Data Protection Act is required.

■ This application enables appropriate processes to be established, such as those for contingency planning and customer service.

MANAGEMENT TECHNIQUES FOR THE MARKETING FUNCTION

LEARNING OUTCOMES

9.63.3 Demonstrate and ability to manage marketing activities as part of strategic implementation.

9.63.4 Assess an organization's needs for marketing skills and resources and develop strategies for acquiring, developing and retaining them.

9.63.5 Initiate and critically evaluate systems for control of marketing activities undertaken as part of business and marketing plans.

4.1 Assess the relevance to an organization of the key concepts of quality management, including structured approaches to continuous improvement and problem solving, and their use in conducting marketing activities.

LEARNING OUTCOMES – CONTINUED

4.2   Develop a plan for compliance of a marketing function's activities with an organization's quality management system.

4.3   Assess the relevance to a marketing function of the concept of process and techniques for process management, and develop a plan for their use in conducting marketing activities.

4.4   Assess the relevance to an organization of the key concepts and techniques of project (or programme) management, and develop plans for their use in conducting marketing and other business activities.

Syllabus References: 9.63.3–9.63.5, 4.1–4.4

Quality and project management

This unit addresses topics which are not usually found in Marketing literature. These are Quality Management and Problem Solving, Process Management and Project Management. These are relevant to the marketing function in two ways:

■ They are directly useful in conducting marketing activities

■ The Marketing Function interfaces with other functional areas with an organization that use these techniques and the application of marketing principles helps to ensure that they have an appropriate customer focus.

KEY DEFINITIONS

Quality management – Quality management is an organization-wide approach focused on continuous improvement, which ensures that the organization's activities meet or exceed customer expectations.

Process management – Process management refers to analysing, monitoring and defining business processes for effectiveness and efficiency.

Project management – Project management is the process of managing non-repetitive activities to ensure that they achieve time, cost and performance objectives.

Definitions of quality

There are two contrasting ways in which Quality may be defined:

■ The economic approach – which says quality is when a product or services satisfies customer wants. Customers make individual assessments of quality, reflecting their needs and wants.

■ The transcendental approach – in which quality refers to innate excellence, or the 'best possible' product or service specification. This underpins views such as that first-class cabins offer better service than other levels on airlines, Mercedes cars are better than Skodas and designer goods are better than chain store goods.

The first of these is, perhaps, more in tune with marketing thinking. This view is underpinned by the work of, for example, Juran, who approached quality from a managerial perspective, focusing on customer requirements.

EFQM model

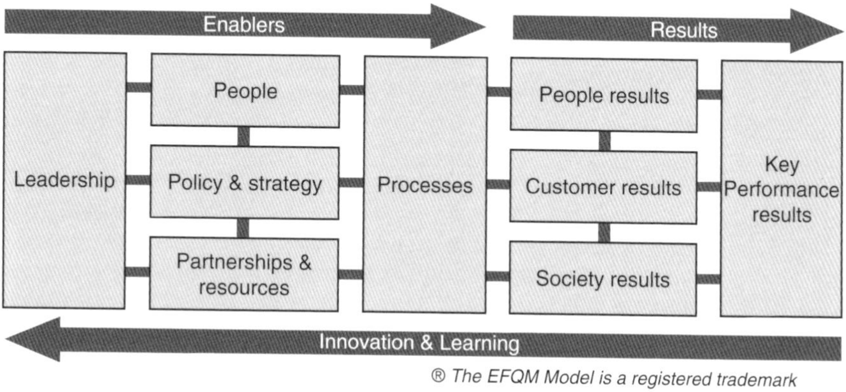

Fig. 7.1.
Source: European Foundation for Quality Management (www.efqm.org)

Techniques for quality management and excellence

Techniques are available to both assess the level of quality – Benchmarking – and to improve processes – Six Sigma.

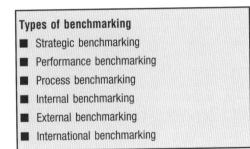

Types of benchmarking

- Strategic benchmarking
- Performance benchmarking
- Process benchmarking
- Internal benchmarking
- External benchmarking
- International benchmarking

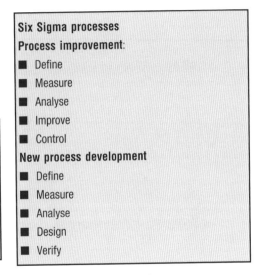

Six Sigma processes

Process improvement:

- Define
- Measure
- Analyse
- Improve
- Control

New process development

- Define
- Measure
- Analyse
- Design
- Verify

Process management v business process improvement

Table 7.1. Process improvement (TQM) versus business process innovation (BPI)

	Improvement	Innovation
Level of change	Incremental	Radical
Starting point	Existing process	Clean slate
Frequency of change	One-time/Continuous	One-time
Time required	Short	Long
Participation	Bottom-up	Top-down
Typical scope	Narrow, within functions	Broad, cross-functional
Risk	Moderate	High
Primary enabler	Statistical control	Information technology
Type of change	Cultural	Cultural/Structural

Source: Davenport (1993)

The service blueprint framework

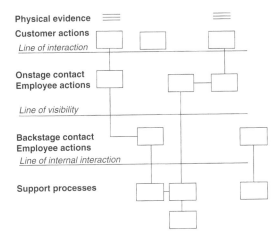

Fig. 7.2.
Source: Zeithaml and Bitner (2003)

Project management

Table 7.2. Checklist for reviewing project planning documents

---

Does the project plan detail:

- What the project and the project management will achieve? (objectives and scope)
- How will the project be managed? (methodology)
- When will the project be complete? (timings)
- Who will do what tasks? (roles and responsibilities)
- When will each task be done? (work breakdown system)
- What resources are required? (resources)
- How much money is required and available? (budget)
- How will the project be evaluated? (evaluation)

Revision tips

■ The concept of quality management is an important one and there is a wide range of views on, and definitions of, what constitutes quality. Ensure that you are familiar with a sample of these.

■ The role of marketing is important in process design as there is an obvious impact on service levels which affect customer loyalty and so, in turn, retention and, ultimately, shareholder value. Make sure that you have relevant examples from your own experience.

■ The role of marketing in the management of processes is also important. Marketing has a contribution to make to the inputs and outputs as well as the transformation produced by a process. Consider processes within your own organization such as New Product Development, Planning and Forecasting. See Question 4 of the December 2006 paper.

■ There are a range of project management techniques which include Gantt Charts, network diagrams and methodologies such as Prince. Again, ensure that you are familiar with these as they represent fertile ground for this examination.

MANAGEMENT TECHNIQUES FOR THE MARKETING FUNCTION

LEARNING OUTCOMES

9.63.3 Demonstration and ability to manage marketing activities as part of strategic implementation.

9.63.4 Assess an organization's needs for marketing skills and resources and develop strategies for acquiring, developing and retaining them.

4.5 Assess the capabilities of an organization to exploit innovation and creativity in its products/services and processes.

LEARNING OUTCOMES – CONTINUED

4.6 Develop and nurture processes and techniques within marketing teams to exploit innovations in marketing.

4.7 Establish a mechanism, which is consistent with organizational policy, for deciding the activities to be undertaken by external suppliers, including agencies and outsourcing, and gain approval for the relevant expenditure.

Syllabus References: 9.63.3, 9.63.4, 4.5–4.7

Innovation and managing external resources

- This unit addresses two important areas. The first is innovation and, in particular, creating an organizational context which encourages it. The second is the use of external resources, focusing on the strategic decisions which impact both directly on profitability and on customer service and consequent indirect impact on profitability.

- It should be revised in conjunction with the material in Unit 9 which looks at the ways in which innovation performance may be measured.

- Innovation is a source of competitive advantage and, as such, is also an important element of the Strategic Marketing Decisions module.

KEY DEFINITIONS

Innovation gap – The innovation gap is the ability of an organization to achieve its innovation requirements. This can be expressed in terms of the failure of the organization to create new ideas and launch successful new products, or in financial terms, detailing the amount of money required from innovation to achieve growth targets.

The difference in performance between organizations or countries in their ability to innovate (from benchmarking studies) is also an innovation gap.

Innovation culture – An innovation culture is an organizational culture where innovation is a central value, and where employees work together to create and sustain innovation within a supportive and productive environment.

Outsourcing – Outsourcing is a general term to describe any activities which are undertaken by an external party. More specific definitions state that outsourcing is a fixed-term contractual arrangement for external work to be undertaken to defined standards.

The financial imperative for innovation

The Innovation Gap can be defined as the difference between revenue from a company's current level of innovation and the revenue required from innovation to achieve growth. It can be calculated in three steps, by assessing:

1. **Basic factors** – which include the company's current annual revenue, desired annual revenue growth and desired cost reductions.

2. **Gap factors** – which review the growth required from new products or services, the amount of existing revenue at risk from failing to create new products (i.e. the revenue lost by failing to exploit new opportunities), savings attainable only through new methods of operating, and the likelihood of an unforeseen event and its impact on revenue.

3. **Results** – which look at the projected revenue, the level of this at risk from gaps in growth, failure to exploit opportunities, cost containment and disruptive changes to determine the revenue required from innovation. This is calculated as a percentage of next year's revenue goal, which is then compared with an estimated innovation capacity which predicts what you may be able to deliver.

Organizational performance in innovation

Factors that assist in innovation include geographical competition, investment and company size and specialism. In addition to the checklist on this page, which can be considered as a diagnostic tool, refer also to the Innovation Audit covered in Unit 9.

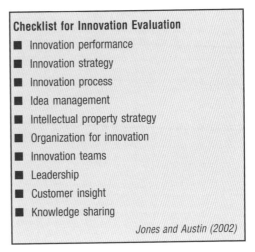

Checklist for Innovation Evaluation
- Innovation performance
- Innovation strategy
- Innovation process
- Idea management
- Intellectual property strategy
- Organization for innovation
- Innovation teams
- Leadership
- Customer insight
- Knowledge sharing

Jones and Austin (2002)

Nurturing successful innovation
Innovation capacity or capability

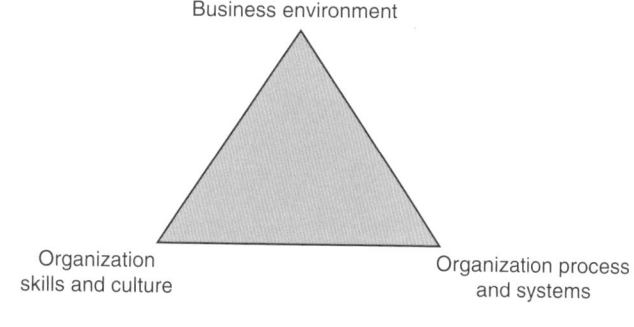

Fig 8.1.

Establishing an innovation culture

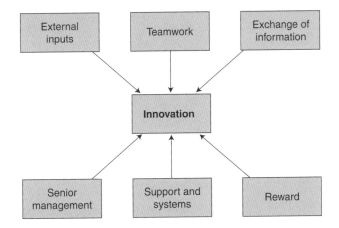

Fig 8.2. Generating innovation
Adapted from Drummond and Ensor (2001)

Outsourcing

Table 8.1. Top 10 reasons for outsourcing

1. Reduce and control operating costs
2. Improve company focus
3. Gain access to world-class capabilities
4. Free internal resources for other purposes
5. Resources are not available internally
6. Accelerate reengineering benefits
7. Function difficult to manage/out of control
8. Make capital funds available
9. Share risks
10. Cash infusion

Source: Managing Marketing Performance
Coursebook – taken from www.outsourcing.com

Deciding to use external suppliers

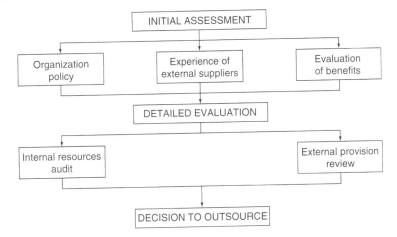

Fig. 8.3.

Outsourcing opportunities

Outsourcing strategies

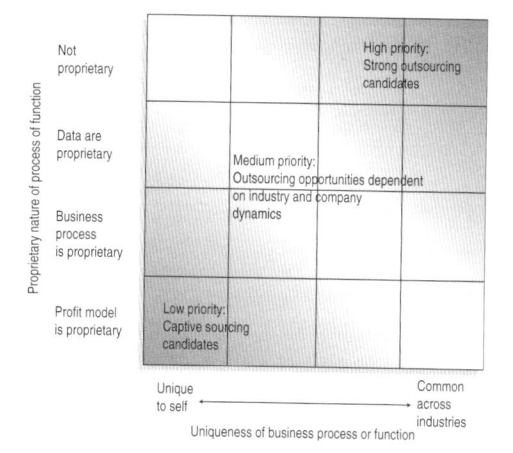

Fig. 8.4.
Source: Gottfredson, M. *et al.* (2005)

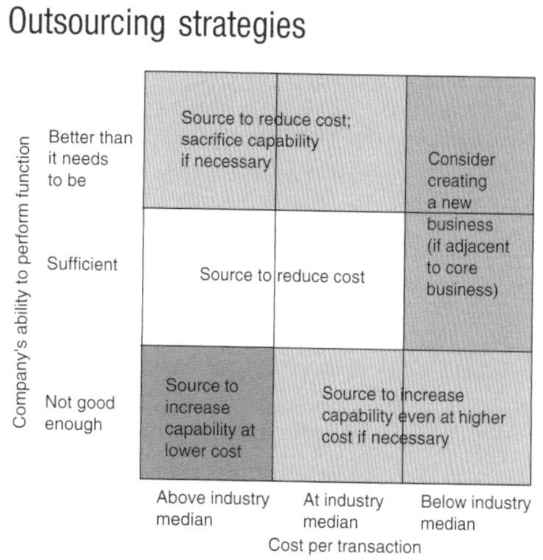

Fig. 8.5.
Source: Gottfredson, M. *et al.* (2005)

Revision tips

■ The starting point for developing an innovation strategy is an innovation audit. Ensure, therefore, that you are familiar with the process and metrics in Unit 9.

■ Remember that this module is about the role of Marketing in establishing an organizational environment which will improve performance. The emphasis, therefore, should be on developing the strategy to create that environment and managing the change process to implement that strategy rather than on the details of, for example, the New Product Development process.

■ In respect of Outsourcing, there are a number of important aspects to consider: what to outsource and the process and criteria for selecting suppliers. Again, however, the strategic implications are important ones to focus on. You should consider the benefits that Outsourcing may bring, for example competitive advantage or knowledge transfer through using specialist external expertise.

■ Note the integration of these topics with other earlier ones. Innovation with Change Management and Outsourcing with Communications, for example. The emphasis in the examination is very much on the candidate's ability to synthesise and apply two or three theoretical concepts and evaluate the outcomes.

MEASUREMENT, EVALUATION AND CONTROL

Unit 9

LEARNING OUTCOMES

9.63.5 Initiate and critically evaluate systems for control of marketing activities undertaken as part of business and marketing plans.

5.1 Develop and use 'accounting' measures of the performance of marketing activities against objectives.

5.2 Define and use customer-related and innovation measures as part of the organization's balanced scorecard.

5.3 Measure the financial returns achieved on specific investments in marketing activities and programmes and compare them with the original business case or investment appraisal.

5.4 Propose measures of the value generated by developing a position based on sustainability or ethics and of the progress of the organization in achieving the desired position.

5.5 Assess the value that marketing activities generate and contribute to shareholder value, as appropriate working with colleagues from other disciplines, using appropriate models and techniques.

Syllabus References: 9.63.5, 5.1–5.5

Measurement, evaluation and control

This is an extremely important unit as it sets out a range of metrics applicable to marketing activities and explains when it is appropriate to apply them.

■ Marketing activities frequently require investment in intangible assets, the benefits of which may not be immediately apparent. In order to justify such investment, these benefits must be quantified. Shareholder value analysis provides a means of achieving this.

■ Taking this approach a step further, Kaplan and Norton's Balanced Scorecard provides a framework which allows activities to be discussed and harmonised across the functions of an organization, objectives set and outcomes measured.

■ There is still, however, an important role for traditional accounting metrics as well as for marketing metrics such as productivity and innovation performance.

KEY DEFINITIONS

Goal – general statement of aim or purpose.

Objective – Quantification (if possible) or more precise statement of the goal (Johnson and Scholes, 1999, p. 14). It should be measurable and time bound, e.g. to be completed at the end of the planning year.

Balanced scorecard – Balanced scorecards combine both qualitative and quantitative measures, acknowledge the expectations of different stakeholders and relate an assessment of performance to choice of strategy (Johnson and Scholes, 1999, p. 468).

Brand equity – A set of assets and liabilities linked to a brand's name and symbol that add to or subtract from the value provided by a product or service to a firm and/or that firm's customers (Aaker, 1998, p. 173).

Absorption costing – A system where all overhead costs are charged to products and services using an allocation base (e.g. a measure of activity or volume such as labour hours) (Collier, 2003, p. 162).

Activity-based costing – Attempts to identify a more accurate basis for overhead cost allocation. Cost pools are used to accumulate the costs of significant business activities and these costs are assigned to products based on cost drivers which measure each product's demand for activities (Collier, 2003, p. 166).

Innovation audit – The Innovation Audit reviews how effectively the organization is able to deliver the level of innovation necessary to create new products, new services and new ways of undertaking activities (Drummond and Ensor, 2001).

Influences on mission and objectives

Fig. 9.1.
Adapted from Johnson and Scholes (1999)

Levels of objectives

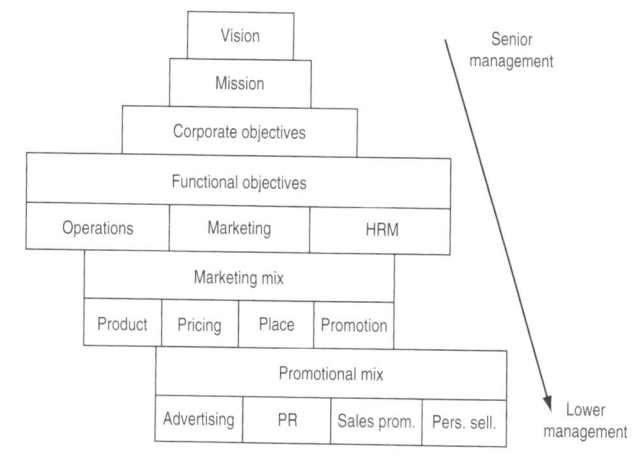

Fig. 9.2.

Goals and objectives – Trade-offs

When developing strategy, trade-offs will be necessary in the majority of decisions at all levels. In setting objectives, the following trade-offs may have to be made.

Trade-offs in setting objectives
- Short-term versus long-term
- Profit margin versus competitive position
- Market penetration versus market development
- Related versus non-related growth
- Profit versus non-profit objectives (social, ethical, environmental, etc.)
- Growth versus stability
- Risk avoidance versus risk taking.

Accounting measures of performance

Table 9.1. The impact of marketing activity on specific element within in the balance sheet

Balance sheet	Marketing variables	Specific examples
Fixed assets		
	Decision to outsource marketing services	Buy in marketing research rather than establish
	Decision to establish in-house marketing services	your own department. Effect would be not to increase fixed assets in this case
	Decision to develop new products	
	Decision to enter new markets	
Current assets		
Inventories	New products	Introduction of new products would increase
Debtors	Promotional decisions	stockholding costs or the build-up of inventories
Cash	Customer service-level decisions	for a promotion would do the same
	Returns policies	
	Efficiency in the handling of customer complaints	Extending credit as part of a promotional decision could increase accounts receivable (debtors). It may also reduce your cash inflows

Current liabilities

Trade creditors | Purchasing policies | Sourcing of materials/merchandise
| Marketing and selling decisions | Decisions taken on what to sell and where to sell. It may affect trade creditors (supplier accounts)

Financed by

Equity | Company-wide decisions regarding the | Entering new markets overseas could involve
Debt | best way to finance new market development | the establishment of new sites (offices,
| or new product development | warehousing, retail selling space, etc.). The company has a choice on how to finance this type of expansion either through increasing its debt (loan financing) or through issuing new shares (equity capital)

Ratio analysis

Table 9.2. Classification of topline financial variables more comments used in strategic planning

Type of ratio

Example topline ratios

1. Profitability ratios

$$\text{Gross profit margin} = (\text{GP/Sales}) \times 100$$
$$\text{Net profit margin} = (\text{NP/Sales}) \times 100$$

Fundamental strength of the business

2. Capital structure ratios, also termed 'gearing' ratios where;

$$\text{Debt ratio} = \text{total debt/total assets}$$
$$\text{Total debt} = \text{current liabilities} + \text{long-term liabilities}$$
$$\text{Total assets} = \text{fixed assets} + \text{current assets}$$

Operational efficiency of the business

3. Liquidity

$$\text{Current ratio} = \text{current assets/current liabilities}$$
$$\text{Liquid ratio} = (\text{current assets} - \text{stock})/\text{current liabilities}$$

4. Asset utilisation

$$\text{Stock turnover ratio} = \text{cost of goods sold/stock at cost on balance sheet}$$
$$\text{Debtor turnover} = \text{sales turnover/debtors}$$
$$\text{credit turnover ratios} = \text{cost of goods sold/trade creditors from the balance sheet}$$

5. Investment performance ratios

$$\text{Price to earnings ratio (i.e. P/E ratio)} = \text{Market price share[1]/earnings per share[2]}$$

[1] From stock market

[2] Declared annually or twice per year by the company

Productivity analysis

Table 9.3.

General formula	Marketing outputs/ Marketing inputs	The general principle is that any output may be expressed as a ratio of any input. The particular variable selected depends on the reason for calculating the productivity ratio
Example 1	Change in sales turnover/Change in communications expenditure	The assumption behind this ratio is that a communications campaign has been undertaken and that this is the sole, or main, reason behind an increase in sales turnover. Additional information must be gathered at the time of collecting ratio data, in order to confirm that another factor has not been the cause of the change. For example, poor distribution by a competitor or a competitor withdrawing from the market.
Example 2	Increase in consumer awareness/Change in advertising expenditure	This provides a useful measure by which to judge, at least in part, the performance of the company. This example is to illustrate that the ratio need not always be purely of financial measures. It may be of a physical and financial measure (see real indices below).

The balanced scorecard

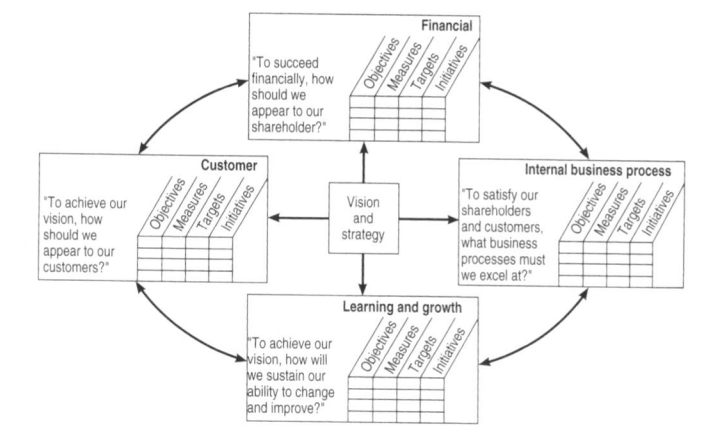

Fig. 9.3.
Source: Kaplan and Norton (1992)

The balanced scorecard

	Strategic objectives	Strategic measures
Financial	F.1 Return on capital F.2 Cash flow F.3 Profitability F.4 Profitability growth F.5 Reliability of performance	⇧ ROCE ⇧ Cash flow ⇧ Net margin ⇧ Volume growth rate vs. industry ⇧ Profit forecast reliability ⇧ Sales backlog
Customer	C.1 Value for money C.2 Competitive price C.3 Customer satisfaction	⇧ Customer ranking survey ⇧ Pricing index ⇧ Customer satisfaction index ⇧ Mystery shopping index
Internal	1.1 Marketing ■ Product and service development ■ Shape customer requirement 1.2 Manufacturing ■ Lower manufacturing cost ■ Improve project management 1.3 Logistics ■ Reduce delivery costs ■ Inventory management 1.4 Quality	⇧ Pioneer percentage of product portfolio ⇧ Hours with customer on new work ⇧ Total expenses per unit vs. competition ⇧ Safety incident index ⇧ Delivered cost per unit ⇧ Inventory level compared to plan and output rate ⇧ Rework
Innovation and learning	I.L.1 Innovate products and services I.L.2 Time to market I.L.3 Empowered workforce I.L.4 Access to strategic information I.L.5 Continuous improvement	⇧ Percentage revenue from pioneer products ⇧ Cycle time vs. industry norm ⇧ Staff attitude survey ⇧ Strategic information availability ⇧ Number of employee suggestions

Fig. 9.4. Objectives and measures
Source: Kaplan and Norton (1992)

The balanced scorecard
Causal relationships

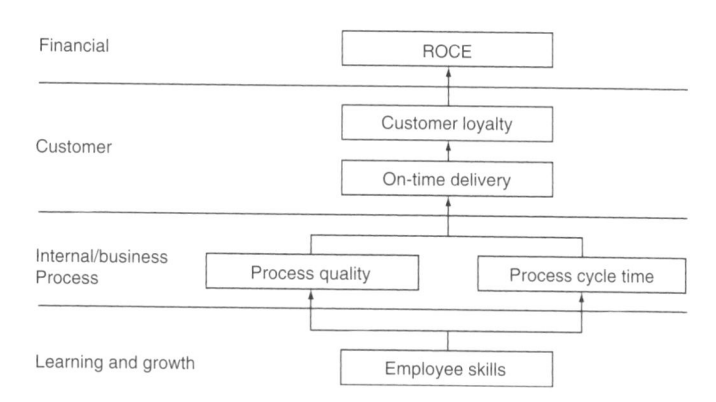

Fig. 9.5.
Source: Kaplan and Norton (1992)

Relationship marketing measures

Little and Marandi (2003) suggest Customer and more specific Relationship areas to be monitored.

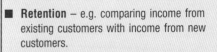

- **Retention** – e.g. comparing income from existing customers with income from new customers.

- **Satisfaction** – e.g. direct measurement of satisfaction as well as monitoring of complaints and the number of complaints.

- **Communication** – e.g. the average number of contacts with customers indirectly using technology or less frequently, in person.

- **Relationship facilitators** – contribute to long-term relationships, e.g. satisfaction and trust.

- **Relationship features** – which describe the nature of the relationship between the supplier and the customer, e.g. customer loyalty.

- **Relationship returns** – literally measure the financial rewards gained by the supplier. One cautionary point suggested by Little and Marandi is that the most satisfied and loyal customers do not necessarily generate the best returns.

Innovation audit

Drummond and Ensor (2001)

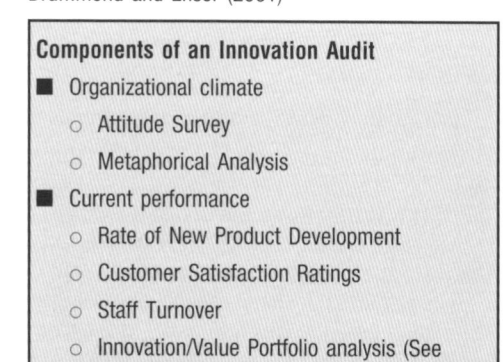

Components of an Innovation Audit
- Organizational climate
  - Attitude Survey
  - Metaphorical Analysis
- Current performance
  - Rate of New Product Development
  - Customer Satisfaction Ratings
  - Staff Turnover
  - Innovation/Value Portfolio analysis (See following page)
- Review of policies and practices to support innovation
- Balance of cognitive styles

The innovation/value matrix

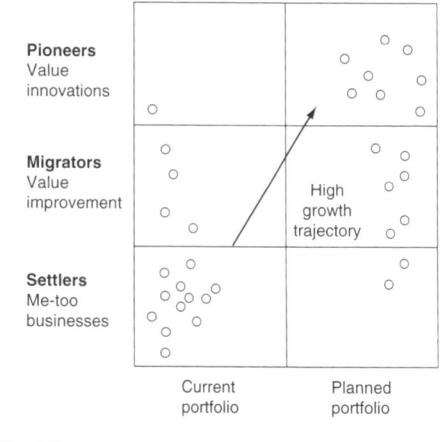

Pioneers
Value innovations

Migrators
Value improvement

High growth trajectory

Settlers
Me-too businesses

Current portfolio

Planned portfolio

Fig. 9.6.
Source: Kim and Mauborgne (1998)

Measuring financial returns on marketing investments

A number of methods are available to appraise investments. Accounting Rate of Return simply calculates the average return on an investment without taking account of the time value of money. Both Discounted Cashflow techniques overcome this disadvantage by applying discount rates (which will usually be provided to you from tables).

The Payback Period technique simply calculates how long it will take to recover the initial investment.

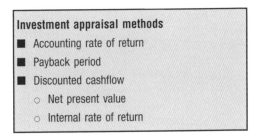

Investment appraisal methods
- Accounting rate of return
- Payback period
- Discounted cashflow
  - Net present value
  - Internal rate of return

Brand valuation

As indicated in Unit 5, there are a number of approaches to brand valuation. Doyle (1998) suggests:

■ Price premium valuation – the price premium over unbranded products is used as the basis for brand valuation

■ Incremental sales valuation – if brands achieve higher sales than unbranded products these incremental sales can be used to value the brand

■ Replacement cost value – the estimated cost of developing a similar brand

■ Stock market valuation – the residual value once physical assets, industry factors and other intangible assets have been removed

■ Future earnings valuation – probably the most appropriate method. This is where the discounted present value of future earnings attributable to the brand is estimated.

Corporate social responsibility
Degrees of corporate, social and environmental reporting

Level of reporting (vertical axis)

5 — **Sustainability development** – Regular externally verified sustainability statement with linkages to environmental and financial data

4 — **Statement** – Regular externally verified reports. True dialogue with stakeholders, indicators, targets, benchmarks and commitment to comprehensive coverage over time

3 — **Report** – Regular report with stakeholder consultation, indicators, financial data, explicit policies and internal systems

2 — **Review** – Occasional descriptive reports addressing different stakeholder needs

1 — **Commentary** – Report of social mission and aims and some descriptive comments

Extent and intensity of coverage

Fig. 9.7.

Shareholder value and marketing Activity

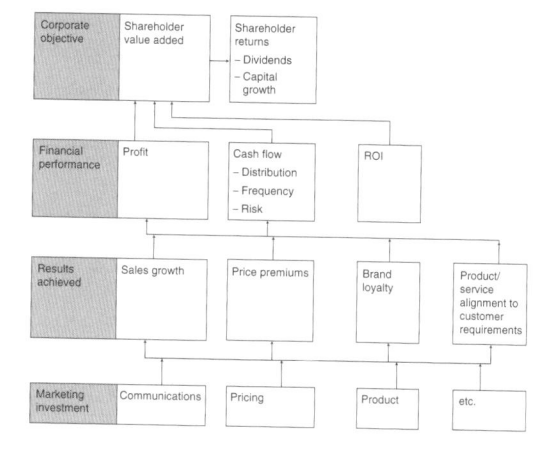

Fig. 9.8.
Adapted from Zadek (1998)

Revision tips

- The concept of Shareholder Value Analysis is that any activity or asset, and so investment in it, should be evaluated in terms of the Net Present Value of the cashflows attributable to that activity or asset.

- When assets are tangible, accountants have developed methods of calculating their value and a number of techniques are set out in this unit.

- Intangible assets, however, are more difficult to value. Consequently, less formal methods of establishing their value have been proposed. These allow a value to be attributed to many marketing assets and a financial case for investment in them made.

- Ensure that you are familiar not only with the various calculations relating to each technique but also to the justification for employing the techniques, their strengths and weaknesses and, therefore, the times when it is appropriate to employ them.

- Ultimately, the objective for any organization is to generate value for stakeholders and, in particular, shareholders. The causal relationships in the Balanced Scorecard effectively deliver Shareholder Value as the ultimate financial outcome and this can provide an outline framework for answers to examination questions. Remember, though, that the Examiners are expecting you to integrate two or three other theory bases with one or other of these to demonstrate your understanding.